The Blaze in the Balkans
Selected Writings 1903-1941

M. Edith Durham

The Blaze in the Balkans
Selected Writings 1903-1941

M. Edith Durham

Edited by Robert Elsie and Bejtullah Destani,
with an introduction by Elizabeth Gowing

In association with
THE CENTRE FOR ALBANIAN STUDIES

Published in 2014 by I.B.Tauris & Co. Ltd.
6 Salem Road, London W2 4BU
175 Fifth Avenue, New York NY 10010
www.ibtauris.com

In association with The Centre for Albanian Studies

Distributed in the United States and Canada exclusively by Palgrave Macmillan,
175 Fifth Avenue, New York, NY 10010

Introduction ©Elizabeth Gowing

The right of Elizabeth Gowing to be identified as the author of the introduction to this work has been asserted by the author in accordance with the Copyright, Designs and Patents Act 1988. The rights of Bejtullah Destani and Robert Elsie to be identified as the editors of this work has been asserted by the editors in accordance with the Copyright, Designs and Patents Act 1988.

All rights reserved. Except for brief quotations in a review, this book or any part thereof, may not be reproduced, stored in or introducd into a retrieval system, or transmitted, in any form or by any means, electronic, mechanical, photocopying, recording or otherwise, without the prior written permission of the publisher.

Typeset by Westrow Cooper in Bembo

ISBN: 978 1 84885 710 0

A full CIP record for this book is available from the British Library
A full CIP record for this book is available from the Library of Congress

Library of Congress Catalog Card Number: available

Printed and bound in Great Britain by TJ International Ltd.

Contents

Introduction by Elizabeth Gowing	ix
The Blaze in the Balkans (1903)	1
My Golden Sisters: A Macedonian Picture (1904)	14
Balkan Sketches: What Use to Make a Fuss? (1904)	25
Balkan Sketches: Life is Cheap (1904)	30
As Others See It: A Sketch in Old Servia (1905)	35
East and West: A Study of Progress (1908)	48
Albanian and Montenegrin Folklore (1912)	55
The Soul of the War (1912)	61
The Advance Guard of the War (1912)	65
Miseria (1912)	69
Hil (1913)	74
Travels in Trueland: An Ecclesiastical Episode (1919)	93
Ritual Nudity in Europe (1920)	106
The Serbs As Seen in Their National Songs (1920)	108

Because of the Berlin Congress: A True Tale, Dedicated to the Drawers of Frontiers (1920)	122
King Nikola of Montenegro (1921)	130
Albania: Oldest and Quaintest of Balkan Peoples (1922)	141
A Bird Tradition in the West of the Balkan Peninsula (1923)	149
Head-hunting in the Balkans (1923)	160
The Balkans as a Danger Point (1924)	166
Tribes of Northern Albania (1925)	179
A Very Free Press (1931)	190
The Making of a Saint (1933)	194
Albania (1941)	199
Bibliography	213

To
Margaret and Pam Davis
With thanks for their support and generosity

Introduction

As others see it is one of the shorter pieces in this rich, provocative collection of the writings of Edith Durham. It could be the title for the whole collection. For this is the dominant preoccupation of Durham, and perhaps of any thoughtful traveller in foreign lands. She is herself the 'other' and the 'others' are also those she is looking on. With such a theme, the editing of the book is well-judged – Bejtullah Destani is a Kosovar Albanian who has lived in London for 19 years, and now represents his native country as Minister Counsellor in Kosovo's first embassy to the UK, he has a fine eye for perspectives on the other. The pieces in the book remind us of the other connections between Britain and the Balkans over recent centuries – of Tennyson, Disraeli, Lord Fitzmaurice, Alexander Thomson, Aubrey Herbert, Margaret Hasluck, Harry Hodgkinson, etc.

With its wide geographical sweep, the book offers a fair picture of the Balkans – Montenegro, Macedonia, Kosovo, Albania, Serbia are all represented – their dangers and wonders, ugly brutality and startling beauty, history, custom, geography, politics. The collection offers vivid pictures of Balkan locations:

the monastery at Gracanica where the crown is tossed three times into the air (like some dangerous bridal bouquet) to decide the heir to the throne (*The Serbs as Seen in their National Songs*), Shkodra which was Durham's home away from home, elegant Cetinje where the Tsaritsa of Russia set up her Girls' School), the rural poverty of mountain Albania (*Hil*, a piece which stays long in the memory though it is not original – in its depiction either of Albania or of poverty – but is a neat personalised reminder of the basic facts of life which still determine human behaviour in the Balkans, and elsewhere today. It shares something with Migjeni's powerful short stories of the area).

But as Durham knows so well, and as we are reminded in the final sentence of *Balkan Sketches*, 'it all depends on the point of view'; this book also thus offers a portrait of the writer. A rounded understanding of M. Edith Durham emerges from the pages. Now she is the reluctant humanitarian (*My Golden Sisters*), now the brave adventurer (*The Blaze in the Balkans*), now academic (*The Serbs as Seen in Their National Songs*) now playful satirist (*Travels in Trueland*). Sometimes she is, herself, the subject of anthropological attention (following a description of the costume of the women in Macedonia she notes 'They wonder at my cordlessness and I at them'. In Kosovo, 'My hat alone was sufficient attraction, for I was the only woman in the land who possessed one. Whence I came from, my relations, and many highly personal details were an unfailing source of interest'). Throughout, she is unsentimental, practical, someone who didn't suffer fools gladly, and took risks in her stride.

To read in *The Soul of the War* of the conditions in which this Hampstead watercolourist stayed in Northern Albania is to gain new respect for her fortitude - 'we lived together, crowded like wild beasts upon straw, in half-burnt houses. Daily they went out to slaughter, returning with blood upon their feet, to hack with a sword bayonet the sheep roasted whole, which formed almost our sole diet... It was a hideous life of blood and muck.' Sometimes, perhaps, her descriptions are exaggerated - comparison of the version of her visit to the monastery at Deçan with letters she sent at the time suggests that in the published account she enjoyed elaborating the extent of potential dangers (or perhaps that she was down-playing these in her letters for the peace of mind of the folks back in London?).

She is almost always balanced in her presentation of the apparent barbarity of the foreigners she describes, offering careful corrective to any suggestion that the British might manage their lives any better. In part, this comes through repeated reminders that Britain was one of the Great Powers which mangled the drawing of Balkan borders which have so hindered progress in the region. But she also shows a healthy disrespect for British ways of working; just as we are being led to patronising despair at the primitive use of propaganda in nineteenth-century Montenegrin nationalist song (*King Nikola of Montenegro*), she damns our civilised ways in the same stroke, 'the minstrel...was the mediaeval forerunner of the cinema - a means by which propaganda may be spread with a minimum of mental exertion on the part of the audience.' Ouch. Similarly, when in *Tribes of Northern Albania* she describes the barbaric-sounding 'blood tax', she preempts any self-righteous sense of Western superiority we might be tempted to feel with the reminder that it is, 'a system which is far more just than the system of "reparations" in force in the rest of Europe, where the victor may extort what he can'. In *The Golden Sisters,* whose eponymous women she has described as 'slow-witted' and 'animal-like', she ends the piece 'Europe still clings to the belief that the Sultan can be taught to govern justly, and alas, it is almost as hard to drive a new idea into Europe as into my golden sisters.' She laments in *Balkan Sketches* 'The Western habit of forming bogus companies by which widows and orphans are robbed of their little all is far more reprehensible than occasional brigandage... "Your brigands have often been to university, and they rob to obtain luxuries. You have had all the advantages of civilisation and education for years, and this is what you do."'

Most powerful of the pieces for me is *My Golden Sisters* with its honest picture of the struggles, frustrations, revulsions and potentials of relief work. It's the account that Oxfam never gives of such activities. It's a world away from Hampstead. Her strength in vignettes through the well-chosen detail comes through. It is the same skill that fixes King Nikola in our mind – 'he was picturesque, he was kindly, and he was courteous. He asked the peasant woman how her pigs were; and at Easter had red eggs in his breeches pockets for the tribesmen.'

It is a favourite pastime of modern-day Balkan commentators to extract lines of political commentary on the region written a generation, fifty, or a hundred years ago and repeat them with a grim nod to 'how true it still is'. This collection of Durham's work reminds us that the truths which still pertain about the Balkans one hundred years after her visits, are not only political. From personal experience I can only reinforce her bid 'to those who have the enterprise to go to Albania to collect the ancient lore that still remains, I would say that though a certain amount of roughing it must be put up with, the welcome that the traveller meets with more than makes up for it. The scenery of the mountains is second to none in Europe.' Equally, my experience working with the craftsmen of a Kosovar filigree co-operative prompts me to echo her description and sense of threat to the silversmiths who 'brought their work to high perfection' (*Albania; Oldest and Quaintest of Balkan Peoples*) in countries where 'these beautiful home industries are fast disappearing before the rush of trashy and cheap machine-made goods'.

The collection shows the reasons why the Albanians so love Durham, their Queen of the Mountain People, who offered humanitarian relief and lobbied for their nationalist cause. But it also explains the reasons King Nikola of Montenegro loved her (he gave her a golden medal, which she was later to return), that the Serbs loved her (the Serbian Archbishop in Prishtina called her 'the greatest friend of Servia'), and the reason that twenty-first century Britain should love her - an independent woman before her time who was an acclaimed ambassador to forgotten peoples in a forgotten part of Europe.

Elizabeth Gowing,
Port Isaac

The Blaze in the Balkans

The Balkans are ablaze again, and the much vaunted Turkish reforms have proved to be as ineffectual as any one who has travelled among any of the Balkan peoples knew they would. Is it likely that the Turks, who have hopelessly mismanaged the enslaved races for five centuries, would suddenly find out how to remedy the accumulated evils of all these years because Austria and Russia told them they must! Is it not a case of "physician, heal thyself"? With their notoriously corrupt system of government, how can any person believe that the Turks, even if willing, are capable of spreading sweetness and light in this unhappy land? Whether the present uprising proves abortive or not is not the question. The point to consider is that as long as the Turk is permitted to "govern" these peoples at all, so long will there be "trouble in the Balkans," and the story will be written in blood, and in more blood, until the end. The population may be crushed into a semblance of quietude temporarily, but there will be no peace, no progress, no civilisation; and it must be remembered that nothing ever stands still. Things that do not progress slip backwards and the longer these people remain under Turkish power, the more demoralised do they become. Those who now denounce them as savages remember that they have had five centuries of Turkish rule. During those five centuries West Europe has advanced, the Near East has rotted, hopeless and helpless. West Europe has lately shuddered, and rightly, at the assassination Servia, and in its horror forgets the school that Servia was educated in. Servia became a Turkish province in the fifteenth century, and was not freed till the nineteenth. None of the nations who helped to retain the Turk in power a right to throw stones. I do not wish to deny the Turk any good qualities. He possibly did the best he was capable of according to his lights. But his greatest admirer must admit that, as an administrator and as a trainer and teacher of subject races, he has failed most dismally.

I have but a fortnight ago returned from the Balkan Peninsula. It was my fifth visit. I have a good many acquaintances of various nationalities, and they talked freely to me, more freely, indeed, than was really at all prudent. They told me, among other things, that as soon as the harvest was in, which would be about the middle of August, a wide-spread uprising would take place, and that it was all fully organised, and they warned me if I were staying out there, not to travel by train on Turkish territory, or, at any rate, in no train that carried Turkish troops. Just at the time that I was told this, I received a copy of the *Times,* in which I read that the outlook in Macedonia was brighter and things were quieting down. I mentioned this to a Bulgarian, and he smiled grimly: "Your people don't know anything about us. Tell them so when you go back." Another man told me, laughing, that the newspaper correspondents had all left Uskub, and that most of them had returned to their respective lands. "They think it is all over," he said, "and it is now really going to begin!" And the belief that it was to be the beginning of the end was widespread among all classes and nationalities. Servian, Bulgarian, Montenegrin, and Christian Albanian alike jeered at the reforms, and asked me if my people really thought them possible. The only reform possible, they agreed, was to remove the Turk altogether from Europe. There are few points upon which the Bulgarian, the Servian, and the Albanian do agree, but upon this point they are at one. Moreover, the situation is so bad that they all think almost any change would be for the better, and they believe that the change is about to take place. Some of the town Christian Albanians, who suffer considerably from the savagery of their mountain brethren, even expressed a desire to be "taken" by somebody. "By whom?" I asked. "Oh, by Austria, or Italy, or you, or anybody. It could not be worse than it is now!"

There is another point on which all the Balkan peoples agree, and that is in their hatred of all Germans, the "dirty Schwabs" as they call them. The Sultan is believed to have obtained up-to-date artillery from Germany though unable to pay for it, and the Emperor is held responsible. "He is a holy Christian man," they say, "and supports the Mohammedans." There was a good deal of Anglophobia in Germany a little while ago; but I doubt if it can have exceeded in bitterness the feeling against the Germans in the Balkan Peninsula. And this feeling in the majority of cases includes the Austrians.

I am always most kindly received, but I am told "Your people have acted very wrongly throughout. Of course we know they had their political reasons, but they acted wrongly.

and in the end will get no good by it." On arrival in a new place, though all my relations consider me aggressively British, I am invariably taken for a Russian, so I make a favourable first impression. And when I ask the reason for this mistake in my nationality I am always told, "because thou comest as our friend," or "because no one else would take so much trouble for us!" Both of which replies are illuminating. Most of the people seem to consider England's position with regard to the Near Eastern questions due to ignorance and not to wilful wickedness such as they ascribe to the Germans. This, however, may be out of kind consideration for my feelings.

The idea of English ignorance is very general. An Albanian one day, to whom I had been talking for quite half an hour, asked me what land I came from.

"I'm English," I replied. "English!" he cried with amazement, that is impossible." "Why?" "Because the English don't know anything!" This is an alarmingly sweeping statement. Nevertheless it is quite true that few English people are aware of the immense strides that have been made in the lands released from Turkish rule in 1878. It is no exaggeration to say that in that short space of time more has been done towards improving all the conditions of life than in the previous four centuries. There are good roads, well-appointed schools, the towns have been largely rebuilt, and they are clean and tidy; far cleaner than those, for example, of Normandy. The free Balkan States are supposed by the average Briton to be wild and dangerous places. I can only say, from experience, that both Servia and Montenegro have treated me exceedingly well, and that to go from either of them into Turkey is to plunge from safety and civilisation into danger; from the twentieth century into the Middle Ages; off the pavement into the sewer.

Owing to local influential friends and a chapter of lucky accidents, too long to relate here, I succeeded but a few weeks ago in penetrating a dark and little known corner of that Turkish province known as "Old Servia." I entered it over a frontier that was lately bleeding, by a pass opened by recent fighting and untraversed for some years by any traveller from the West of Europe. I have no space here to recount the journey along a track marked with murder stones into this helpless, hapless land. I started upon the expedition with gay light-heartedness; but I was conscious almost as soon as I had crossed the frontier that there was horror in the air. Every one of the Christian population was afraid of an indefinite something which might happen any minute; there was a curious sensation of mistrust everywhere. I had started with the idea that there was no danger, and was somewhat surprised when every one said "Fear not. To-day it is safe." By way of cheering me some women said, "The Turks are afraid of your friends across the frontier. They will not dare touch you for they know you would be nobly avenged." This latter, of course, was nonsense, but they believed it. The local point of view was illustrated with peculiar vividness by the conversation of the women. They were extremely ignorant; England was a mere name to them that conveyed no idea at all. Beyond their own immediate surroundings, indeed, they had no ideas, and their whole mental horizon was bounded by Turks. "Turks," I must here state emphatically means throughout the Balkan Peninsula "Mohammedans." A Mohammedan of any race calls himself and is called a Turk. These women used to come in to interview me, for I was a stranger and quite a new sight. My hat alone was sufficient attraction, for I was the only woman in the land that possessed one. Whence I came from, my relations, and many highly personal details were an unfailing source of interest. Truth to tell, these conversations, when one arrives tired after a long day's ride, are wearisome to the last degree, but in travelling in these lands there is only one road to success, and that is not to lose patience with the people under any circumstances. Omitting many personal questions about myself, both inside and outside, the conversation was always on this pattern. "Have you a father?" "No." "Did the Turks kill him?" "No." This seemed to cause surprise. Then, "Have you any brothers?" "Yes." "Glory be to God! How many Turks have they killed?" My expedition was looked on as a rather sporting event; consequently my male relatives were credited with a passion for the battlefield, which they are far from possessing. There was always some disappointment when I said they had slain none, and a feeling that the family was not up to sample. The next question would be, "Is thy villayet (= province) far off?" "Yes, very." "Five days?" "More." "God help thee! Are there many Turks in thy villayet?" "No, none." "No Turks! Dear God, it is a marvel!" and so on, and so on. "The Turks," said a man to me, "shot my father before my eyes when I was fifteen." His wife gave a cry of alarm, and rushed to shut the window lest she should be overheard. And all these things are trivial details, but little straws show which way the wind blows. To me they were more eloquent than columns of unauthenticated atrocities in the papers.

The land, until lately terrorised and plundered by the Mohammedan Albanians, was being eaten up by a large army of occupation, and hay and corn were dear. I saw quantities of soldiers. Some 30,000 Nizams were encamped in the neighbourhood of one town and 50,000 in the next district, so I was told. The people were in terror of the Nizams; but they were in even greater terror of the Mohammedan Albanians. "When the Nizams go, the Albanians will attack as again. The 'reforms' are nothing." Poor Stcherbina, the Russian consul, who was murdered at Mitrovitza, was looked on as a martyr who had died to save them, and I was shown his photograph. "Till he was shot, the Government would do nothing to protect us. Then Russia made them."

Every one was hopeless and incredulous of reforms, and has ceased to look for help to any Power but Russia. I can best describe the way in which the Christian population regards the Mohammedans by saying that they would not allow me to go into the town of Ipek with less than five men, and that the head of the monastery, at which I was lodging, himself went with me. Whether these precautions were necessary I cannot say. I only know that the people of the monastery were horrified when I proposed going alone with my guide, and begged me not to do it. The town itself is a frowsy hole, too squalid for picturesqueness, a striking contrast to the clean, tidy little towns of Servia and Montenegro.

The fat and fertile plains around, which undulate away as far as Kosovo, could produce much, but, owing to the fact that they are liable to constant raiding and to the other fact that what is not plundered by Albanians is taken by tax-gatherers, they are sparsely inhabited and but scantily cultivated. The houses, which are few and far between, have the appearance of block-houses, and have tiny loophole-like windows. Houses here must be capable of sustaining an attack. The Turkish officials provided me with two mounted gensdarmes, and I rode to the lonely monastery of Decani. Here I met with the striking example of the Christians' opinion of the Nizams. The church, a relic of the days of Servia's glory, is a very fine structure of white marble, and the monastery was one of the richest in the country. Now it is very poor, for the Albanians have swooped upon its lands. Twenty Nizams were quartered in the monastery under the command of a young Turkish lieutenant, for the neighbourhood was accounted dangerous. I was not allowed to go outside the monastery without the gensdarmes. When evening came and I wished to go to bed, I was approached by a young theological student who was attached to the monastery and who had been told off to look after me. He was a gentle, very civil young fellow of Servian blood, who had lived most of his life in the neighbourhood, and had a timid, subdued air. He looked anxious and whispered to me, "Lock your door to-night. The Nizams are from Asia. They are very bad. They will probably come to your room, and they are devils." I had, of course, intended locking the door, Nizams or no Nizams, and I thought he was nervous, so I thanked him and said, "Good night," without paying much attention to his fears. Just as I was about to fasten the door, my guide appeared. He had been recommended to me as a most reliable man, and I had every confidence in him. He came softly down the corridor, entered my room, and tried the iron bars at the windows. Finding them strong, he then examined the lock on the door and the large staple the bolt shot into, and ascertained that the key would turn twice. Then he said, "Lock your door and turn the key twice. The Nizams will come in the night. They are very bad. They come from Asia. They all have long knives. They will come in the night, and they will do—so!" he drew his finger across his carotid, dropped his head on one side, and gave a clicking gasp that was horribly realistic and must have been studied from nature; "they will kill you for what you have in your saddle-bag; they will say the Christians have done it, and the officer will believe them."

He waited outside till I had double-locked the door, said "sleep safely," and left me. I had no weapon of any kind with me, so I reflected that surgical operations, of the above violent description, were better done under chloroform, and went to sleep. As I was very tired, I slept through till morning, and I shall never know if that door was tried. I fancy the danger was exaggerated, as most people are governed by expediency, and the game would not have been worth the trouble. I tell the episode as it happened, to show the estimation in which the army of the reformers is held. Next morning I made the acquaintance of the officer. He was much exercised about me and agog with curiosity. To judge from the embarrassment it caused him, I think it must have been one of the first times he had interviewed an unveiled lady. He was a civil, gentlemanly young fellow, and very anxious to talk with me. Unluckily he spoke nothing but Turkish, of which I know no word and the conversation was interpreted by one of the gensdarmes. I cannot therefore vouch for the truth of it. It was reported thus: He came from Stamboul, and was in this part of the Empire for the first time. He asked if I knew Stamboul, and on learning that I did not, said he was very sorry that I should not have been there first. There all peoples and all religions lived together in peace, as they do in your land; all was good and happy. Here it was not so. He himself was amazed to find it so wild. He had not known there were such savages in the land. The Albanians were a great surprise to him. Here some one intervened and told him that they were by no means new to me, and that I had previously been in Albania. Thereupon he asked for my opinion on them and the political situation. I left the political situation alone, and said, "The Albanians are very brave and have plenty of intelligence, but they know nothing, and they live like animals." He agreed at once, and said with emphasis, "They must be taught, they must have schools; schools in every town and in every village; schools everywhere." I reflected that, as the Turks have held Albania for quite four hundred years, it was a pity they had not thought out some plan of this sort a little earlier in the day, but I merely remarked that schools were certainly required.

I was then told that the lieutenant was much pleased with my views, and said that the English understood Turkey. He was kind enough to add that the Sultan, the King of England, and the Emperor of Germany were the only sovereigns in Europe who had intelligence. My feelings at the company that was allotted us were too deep for words, but I believe the gendarme filled the gap with something that expressed the joy that I was supposed to feel. By the influence of these three sovereigns, said the lieutenant, order would be brought about throughout Turkey. He seemed to be blissfully unaware that

All the king's horses and all the king's men,
Can never put Humpty Dumpty together again.

He was very sanguine about the "reforms," and seemed to think they were well on the way to completion. And all the time the Christians of the monastery sat round and said nothing, and all the time I thought of the outbreak which I had been told was preparing. And the lieutenant babbled on. In order that I might see for myself how reformed the country was, he proposed that I should go yet further afield. "Take as many of my Nizams as you wish and go to Gusinje," he said "instead of returning the way you came." Now this was a very tempting offer, for Gusinje has the worst reputation of all the towns of North Albania, and few people from the West have succeeded in penetrating it. But the officer did not offer to accompany me, and I remembered the warnings of the night before. Moreover, to prevent my further explorations the Pasha at Ipek had detained my passport, and to be caught up-country, minus a passport, by a Turkish official might lead to very unpleasant consequences. But I badly wanted to go. I looked at my guide's face for the casting vote, and the haggard anxiety of it decided me at once. I politely declined the offer and he breathed again. Safe back in England I feel as though I had thrown away an opportunity, but, excepting that young Turkish officer, every one, including even the gendarme who escorted me back to the frontier, assured me that it would have been an expedition from which I should never have returned. I have not sufficient experience of Nizams to offer an opinion.

The lieutenant very politely escorted me back to Ipek, this time with five mounted gensdarmes. He pointed out how well I was being taken care of, and begged that I would tell my people of the improved state of the country. I must therefore emphasize the fact that it was possible, protected by five armed men, to ride for three hours without being shot at, for this was the fact he so greatly admired.

Briefly, the "reforms," as far as "Old Servia" is concerned, consist of a large army of Nizams, of which the inhabitants are terrified, and for which they have to pay. This has, by force of arms, temporally ejected the Mohammedan Albanians. These soldiers, I was told, were unpaid and insufficiently fed. And even some of the Christians spoke of them with more or less pity on this account, much as they disliked and feared them. In Albania, so far as I could learn from the Albanians, nothing that is likely to lead to any future improvement has been affected. Without making war upon them, the Turks cannot disarm the wild mountain tribes. Moreover, in the event of a war with Bulgaria, Turkey would require these same men as soldiers, and, as the bulk of the unruly ones are Mohammedans, would probably obtain them; but such is the strained situation that this is not quite certain. So valuable, indeed, have they always been as fighting men, that the Turkish Government has hitherto allowed them every licence in order to keep on good terms with them, and nothing but Austro-Russian pressure has brought about even a pretence at keeping order. The Albanians are a fiercely independent people, and have hitherto tolerated Turkish "government" only because it is unable to govern them. They have formed hitherto, the flower of the Turkish army in Europe and in return for their services have been allowed to do as they please. I found many people who believed that in the event of a general war it was possible that the Albanians would elect to play a game of their own, and not to support a dying cause. Some, including Albanians, even spoke of "the Albanian king that is soon to be." I cannot say that I see any likelihood that this wild scheme will be carried out. Nevertheless, I was surprised to find many Serbs in favour of it. They believed that all Albanian atrocities were instigated by the Turkish

Government, and that, left to themselves, the Albanians would develop into a fine people. That they have many fine qualities is undoubtedly true. Whether they are capable of government is quite another thing. To this I was always given the old reply, "things could not be worse than they are now."

As far as Old Servia and Albania are concerned the reform scheme is a mere farce; neither has it been more successful in Macedonia. The "reforms" are offered many years too late in the world's history, and all the Balkan peoples know how much Turkish promises are worth. In fact, when one is in the Balkan Peninsula, all plans for a reformed and peaceful Turkish Empire in Europe, no matter how well they read on paper in England, resemble nothing so much as attempts to solder up a volcano in eruption.

"Europe," said a man to me, "knows nothing about us, cares nothing, understands nothing. If no one will help us we must help ourselves. The organisation in Macedonia is complete. We have, and have had for years, agents in every town, in every village. We are fully armed. The people are ready to die for the cause. All is ready, and we begin."

This was in July, and they have begun. If the rest of the schemes that I got wind of are carried out with the same punctuality, a good deal of "history" is hurrying up. I have seen too much of the Balkan people to offer any solution of their difficulties, for there is "a lion in every path." But I have found them honest, kindly, generous and hospitable, and I wish them well.

[from: *The Monthly Review*, London, Vol. 12, September 1903, p. 54-65.]

My Golden Sisters:
A Macedonian Picture

They are stumpy, they are stout, they are heavily built and clumsy, they have faces like Dutch cheeses; they near their hair in two draggly, skimpy pigtails which they prolong with wool and string and ornament with a bunch of brass buttons, the handle of a broken pair of scissors, a bunch of steel chain, or some obsolete Austrian coins; they tie their heads up in black handkerchiefs which cover mouth and chin in Mohammedan manner, and their costume is the most unlovely ever yet devised; they call me their "golden sister." The yard is full of them, and they are all unutterably filthy.

"Give, give," they cry from morning till night. They seize me as I pass, and I keep my hands in my pockets to save them from unwashen kisses. "I have received nothing," cries the first, "nothing, nothing. Oh, my golden sister, tell them to give to me." "Is thy village burnt?" "All burnt, all burnt." "Then thou hast received flour?" (This sternly). "I receive flour," she admits reluctantly. "Give me thy ticket." A glance at this shows that she has also had a blanket. This, too, she admits. And a *mintan* (wadded coat). All these she has had some days ago. "But to-day nothing, nothing." "Go, there is no more for thee. Thou hast received enough."

She is indignant. Another woman, she says, has received linen for a shirt. It is useless to point out that her own shirt is in good condition, whereas the other lady is in rags. She knows that the depot possesses linen, and linen she has made up her mind to have. I pay no further attention to her,—there are a hundred others to interview—but she remains for hours. She is still there when I return from visiting the sick and her cry is continually, "I have received nothing." She expects a gift every time she visits the depot, and she will return again and again to the charge.

The funds of the society do not permit of our giving a garment to every member of a family, and the most able-bodied usually takes possession of the coveted article. A stout and comfortable woman, warmly clad in the multitude of wadded upper garments in which they like to wrap themselves even in warm weather, prayed eloquently for a *mintan* for her daughter. "She is very cold, very cold; she has nothing; all night and all day she is cold."

"But we gave you a *mintan*." She points complacently to the one she has on. We laugh, and tell her to lend it her daughter, and the mere idea makes her very indignant.

Orphans are known to be the recipients of special relief. "I have no father," says an elderly married woman as a reason why she should receive another gift; and a man of fifty thinks he would like to go to the proposed American Orphanage. An anxious woman with a child of five years comes forward and begs for some physic to make it speak. It is a deaf-mute, and we cannot make her believe that we are powerless to assist.

Peasants that are obviously in want, lean and ragged, we assist, even though their village be not burnt. These receive a gift of flour and depart with thanks. They are, as a rule, much more grateful than those who are on the list, and have been receiving a regular grant for weeks. One poor old lady threw up her hands to heaven and crossed herself before taking up her little sack. Some burst into tears, and one old widow to whom I gave money wished me as many blessings as she had hairs on her head, and all that my heart desired. The last she emphasised by patting her abdomen. Others, I regret to remark cheerfully, "Now I want a blanket, a *mintan*, linen for a shirt and stockings." Not so the two brides, dumpy and shapeless maidens, overpowered with exceeding shyness, whose marriage coffers, filled with the work of years, have been plundered by the Turks. They pray only for a piece of stuff to make a garment, and are so overcome by the gift of a good length of cloth apiece that one weeps tears of joy, and both overwhelm us with thanks.

One woman put in a blood-curdling claim for help the other day. She admitted at once that her village had neither been burnt nor plundered, but she said that the Turks had roasted her husband to death in an oven, and that she was quite destitute. She stated the fact crudely and without adornment, and her manner inclined me to belief. Gruesome things have been done in this land before now, and of excessive flogging, when a search is made for arms, there is plenty of evidence. I gave her privately a gift of money, as a sack of flour to one from a village hitherto unaided is apt to bring down the whole village for relief the very next day. This is the only case of the sort that has come to me.

This was all written yesterday. Now the yard is full of more golden sisters from elsewhere, and to-morrow, and to- morrow, and to-morrow there will be yet more. And all alike, so that I can hardly tell "t'other from which," and all bound round the abdomen with some fifteen yards of black woollen cord, knotted up the front so that it projects hideously and forms a sort of shelf, upon which they rest their arms. They tell me that when the cord is off they feel as if they "had lost their souls." They wonder at my cordlessness and I at them. Nevertheless, they have no doubt that I am their sister. For my part, I wonder if they belong to the same genus as I do—let alone species, and a certain nigger song, adapted, flits through my head, "Oh, those golden sisters; oh, those golden sisters; oh, those golden sisters, oh!"

Another woman appears. She declares vehemently, "I have had nothing." She is from a burnt village, and should have received much. Her ticket proves that she has had some of all that we supply. But she persists in her denial. It was another "Madama" who gave her all these things; this one (myself) has given her nothing. She expects a second outfit from me and is left talking. It is astonishing how slow-witted my golden sisters are, and how impossible it is to drive a new idea into them. Animal-like, they have learnt that food is to be found in a certain spot, and they return again and again. They pursue me in the street; they say they have a ticket for flour, and that my servant has refused to give them any. They cry, they shout, they all talk at once. I return to the depôt and ask an explanation. A week ago, it appears, they received rations for a month, and were told not to come again till the month was up. This has all been already explained to them. We explain it again. They begin again, "My golden sister, I have come for flour, and your servant will not give it to me." Renewed explanations; the ticket is shown, read aloud, the day of the month stated, &c. The incident appears closed. But no, as soon as they can get a word in, and rather before, they begin, "Listen, my golden sister; I have come for flour. Your servant, &c. &c." After the fourth or fifth explanation we vainly order them to leave the depot; they all squat in a row and we leave them, and on our return later the chorus again arises. They admit that they have plenty of flour still at home, but until it is time to retire thither they persist in their demand.

Some are extraordinarily persevering. We have hired rooms for sick people from time to time. There is a woman in the town who had a wounded man staying in her house before the British Relief Fund was started. She turns up regularly and demands to be paid. She admits that she made the arrangement herself, with no thought of payment at the time, but now, as other women have been paid for rooms she ought to be paid also. She waylays me at the door and waits for me on the stairs; she comes into the hospital with the out-patients; I fly when I see her coming down the street. I have even been reduced to taking her by the shoulders and turning her out, but when I leave the place for good I believe that one of the last things I shall see will be her dirty mauve plush dress and her turn-up nose as she cries, "The other women have been paid for rooms," &c.

The gratitude of my golden sisters can occasionally be more charming than their indignation. They embrace me in a hug of dirty rags, and they kiss me on both cheeks. One poor old lady told me, after this ceremony, that she had been mourning the death of her son for eight years to such an extent that during all of that period she had never washed her head! "No soap," she cried, "will ever touch it again. I mourn always!" I started from her embrace. "That is not clean," I cried rudely. "No, my golden sister," she said, "it is not clean. I mourn always." I felt thankful for the custom that caused her to tie her head up in a handkerchief, and concluded our transactions rather hastily. I fear she was disappointed that her revelations did not produce extra rations.

There are also delicate attentions which I could dispense with. A dog jumped up and made a muddy paw-mark on my jacket, whereupon a woman very kindly rushed to my assistance, spat copiously on the spot, and was about to scour it with her elbow. I shied promptly and thrust out a defensive arm. She was surprised, and I fear hurt in her feelings. So was another woman who told her little boy to kiss my hand. He had diphtheria, and the kiss was to be as thanks for the injection of serum he had just received. As, in spite of my efforts, many people insist on kissing my hand daily, I felt it my duty to keep it as free from infection as circumstances permit, and I refused his homage. My golden sisters have not the smallest thought about infection, either with regard to diphtheria or small-pox. In one village I was asked to give an extra "tip" for the cooking of my supper, because the priest's wife had cooked it for me at her own house, and she was only just recovering from small-pox, and her two children were still ill.

On the other hand, every one is afraid of pulmonary consumption, and it is difficult to get any one even to wash a patient's linen. It is hardly necessary to say that no sanitary precautions of any kind are ever taken. Every description of filth is thrown into the streets on a rainy day to be washed into the lake. There is no other way of disposing of sewage. After rain people drink water that is thick and yellow, "la soupe dysenterique," as the doctor pleasantly calls it. The death-rate is, of course, high, as, in addition to all the usual diseases, gunshot wounds have to be reckoned also. The "coup-de-fusil" is chronic here throughout the year, and becomes epidemic during the summer. When it is raging, it may even be called infectious and contagious, for it is possible to develop a bullet while on the way home from visiting a patient.

Outwardly, of course, my golden sisters have a very great horror of water, and if the doctor order a cold compress, are much alarmed. They seldom take their medicines properly, for there are many difficulties in the way. To begin with, there is nothing with which to measure a dose. You cannot prescribe a tea- or a table-spoonful in a land where the articles don't exist, and the pharmacy does not possess measured bottles. The tiny cups from which black coffee is taken are the only things at all of a standard size, but in the villages only a few families possess them. Moreover, every one believes that the more medicine they take, the sooner they will recover, and they come back triumphantly four days after they have received medicine for a week, to say they have finished it and want more. When they have received a prescription, and I have signed it, much trouble often begins. Nothing will make some women understand that they are to take it to the pharmacy and receive the physic there. "I am a poor woman, I have come for physic, and you have given me nothing." The letter, she is told, will obtain medicine. She is to go to the pharmacy, &c. She does not know where the pharmacy is. It is in the bazar where she goes for business on market-days. If she will go to bazar, any one will show her the pharmacy. She begins again, "My golden brother (this to the doctor), I am a poor woman: I came here for physic," &c. All she has to do, we say, is to go to the bazar. The situation of the pharmacy is elaborately described, and she is sent downstairs. We finish the out-patients. We dress the in-patients and we return to the depôt. There we find the woman with the paper in her hand. She has not been to the bazar; she has made no attempt to find the pharmacy; she has come straight to the depot. "Listen, my golden sister. I am a poor woman. I have come for physic," &c. The bazar is probably full of the folk of her own village, and she will have to go there on her way home, but to the depot she persists in coming, and she begins again. "My golden sister," &c.

Were it not for their extreme poverty and misery, my golden sisters would be intolerable. But they are the wretched and ignorant victims of international jealousies and political hatreds, and one cannot but pity them. Their male folk, who possess only a fraction more intellect, joined a "band," and are now houseless, workless, penniless, and may be wounded also. No member of the band had ever had a gun before: there was not a good shot in it; it was led by the village schoolmaster, who was as ignorant of things military as are my golden sisters of things in general. It made a futile, hopeless attempt foredoomed to failure, and allowed itself to be caught in a narrow valley. It was routed and its village burnt to the ground. Nor did the Committee which urged these men to rise expect more of them than that this blood and suffering should excite the sympathy of Europe. Therefore the more deaths the better.

"We expected to lose half the population in the insurrection," said one who is "behind the scenes" to me, "and we have lost scarcely a quarter." And he seemed disappointed.

And as long as Turkish rule continues, so long will the peasantry arise and make hopeless efforts against it and the tale will be written in blood and more blood till the end. The peasant fears to rise, for he is not "a fighting man," and he knows the probable consequences of failure; but his lot is so intolerable that, as he says himself, he may as well die as live.

The tale of excessive taxation, and of the way in which even double or treble the amount due is forced from the defenceless Christian villager, has been told too often to need recapitulation. In addition to this, he is liable to robbery and brigandage in the wilder parts, for the Turkish Government seldom or never makes any attempt to restrain the lawlessness of a large part of the Mohammedan population. There is no appeal and no redress for the Christian, even when his children are stolen and put up to ransom for such a heavy sum that he has to sell all his flocks and borrow money, to rescue them from the death that would be their fate, should he fail to pay.

The peasant knows nothing at all of the outside world nor of the organisers of the movement that bids him rise. He knows only that the Turks make his life a burden and the Committee will have him shot if he refuses to join a "band." If he joins it there is the off chance of freedom and living happily ever after. This, he believes, means licence to carry a gun and treat the Turks as they have treated him. He rises now to the call of Bulgaria, financed by Panslavonic funds, and he dances to a Bulgarian air. He would have risen equally to the call of Greece or Servia had either of those nations been able to afford to pay the pipes so handsomely, and unless Europe intervenes to save him from his "friends" and foes he will continue to rise as long as there is anything left of him. And Europe says when he rises, "Those that ask shan't have," and when he is quiet, "Those that don't ask don't want."

I cannot pretend that this peasantry is in any way lovable or admirable. As far as I have seen it, it is a peasantry of the lowest type, dull-witted and of poor physique, inferior to any of the other Balkan races with which I am acquainted, and, under the present government it can never by any possibility become any better. The Turkish system of administration is corrupt beyond all cures. No Austro-Russian quack medicines can hurt it. All efforts at patching and mending the rotten structure are foredoomed to failure. They may enable the Turk to reign a little longer in Europe, but they will produce no improvement in the state of the people. Europe is largely responsible for the fact that the Turk is still here and that the subject Christians are corrupt, degraded, and semi-savage. I use the term "savage" advisedly, for I know a man who boasts of having poisoned fifteen Turkish soldiers, and we have been asked at this depôt to supply poison for traitors, it being unsafe to shoot them. The Turks took this land five centuries ago. It is one of the fairest corners of Europe, and they have made it a disgrace to humanity. In point of civilisation it has in many ways advanced very little beyond the point it had reached when Mohammedan rule began here, and it will never advance while that rule continues. A Christian ruler under the supervision of the Powers and not of the Sultan is the only cure for existing evils, and even then progress will be effected but slowly.

Here we wait from day to day, and there is no news of the promised reforms. We begin to doubt whether they were ever intended for anything but a topic of conversation for the Sultan and various envoys. All hope of help is fast dying away and the human shooting season has begun. The disease is only chronic at present, but the number of cases is increasing. Europe appears to demand another bath of blood before she is convinced that decided action is necessary; and there is, as far as I can see, no room for doubt that, should she elect to wait a little longer, her desire will be amply and fully satisfied. Europe still clings to the belief that the Sultan can be taught to govern justly, and, alas, it is almost as hard to drive a new idea into Europe as into my golden sisters.

Ochrida, March 7, 1904

[from: *The Monthly Review*, London, Vol. 15, May 1904, p. 73-81.]

Balkan Sketches:
What Use To Make A Fuss?

Some one knocked at my door early one morning and my youthful interpreter came in with an anxious expression of face. Being a Balkan Christian he has naturally inherited a tendency always to expect the worst. "I think I had better tell you," he began apologetically, "something a little unpleasant has been happening last night." As I was upon Turkish territory, I was, of course, neither greatly surprised nor disturbed by this information; but I confess that, though 'I had been there before,' I was unprepared for the sequel. "Djaffir," he went on, "has been having a trouble with a Turkish soldier."

Now, Djaffir was my kavas, a Moslem Albanian and ex-brigand, who was paid to hang about my premises with a rifle and revolver, to be used, I suppose, against his co-religionists and professional colleagues in case of need. For, though native Christians, with very few exceptions, are forbidden to carry firearms, the Turkish "Government" kindly permits—nay, encourages—foreign Christians to hire armed Moslems to protect them from the possible consequences of its own inability to govern, and there is no difficulty about finding a stalwart

Albanian who is happy to do nothing in a cartridge-belt at your door. Djaffir was a thick-set, tough-looking individual with a singularly inexpressive face, who had interested me but little. I had sent him on a few errands, and had otherwise had little or nothing to do with him.

"It was like this," continued the interpreter. "Djaffir went home to see his wife yesterday, just after sunset. He found his wife very frightened. She said a soldier had come in to rob the house, but she had screamed very loud and he had run away. But still she was very frightened, for she thought he was hiding some- where near, and that he would come back and steal things in the night. Then Djaffir was very angry, for it is a great crime to go into a Moslem house where there is only a woman. He went to look, and there he found the soldier, hiding in the stable."

I expressed surprise that the soldier should have been foolish enough to enter a Moslem house when there were plenty of Christian ones at hand which could have been burgled with impunity.

"Ah, but you see that soldier he was drunk. Of course he must have meant to go to a Christian house. Most likely he was too drunk to know where he had gone. So Djaffir seized hold of him, for he was too drunk to defend himself, and beat him and beat him till he was tired, and then he just threw him out in the street in the dark. He never stayed to see if the soldier was alive, but he came back here to sleep, and in the morning he tells me."

This was a pretty beginning. I summoned the hero of the exploit and asked for further details. He was usually a very unemotional being, but this morning he was a picture of stolid self-satisfaction.

"Would it not have been possible," I inquired, "to have handed the soldier over to justice?" "Oh, yes." But Djaffir greatly preferred inflicting the punishment himself. I suggested that it had been a little violent, and he admitted that he had beaten the man until he was too tired to hit him again; in fact, when he had once begun, he had thought of nothing more till he was exhausted; then he had thrown him out so covered with blood "that no one would have known him." Thus Djaffir cheerfully.

The night patrol, I learned later, had picked up the poor wretch and taken him to the military hospital. I had visions of trials, arrests, law courts, and other unpleasantnesses, complicated by unknown tongues and interpreters, and did not feel particularly happy. Djaflir, however, explained with great sang-froid that there was no danger, "for I hit him hard on the head many times, and he cannot speak." This circumstance appeared to give general satisfaction; we dismissed the subject and returned to our usual occupations.

Two days after we were not so cheerful. My interpreter appeared with a long face. "You know that soldier? Well, it is very bad to-day. He has come to his senses, and has given Djaffir's name!"

"And what has happened?" "Well, Djaffir has been questioned and he has sworn 'How can I have beaten a Turkish soldier when I was with the English Madama all the time?' This is very bad. Now we shall be asked if this is true. What shall we do?" The poor youth was agitated. "I know I am a very bad coward," he said, apologetically. "You see I am a Christian. I do not wish to tell a lie if I am asked. But if I tell the truth,

Djaffir will perhaps be punished, and then afterwards he may be revenged on me and perhaps even on my people. What shall we do?" The situation was indeed sufficiently awkward for him.

"We have not been asked yet," I said. "We will do nothing. We will wait and see." So we waited. Djaffir, who was doubtless aware that we held all the trump cards, remained unperturbed, and another day passed. Then both men became quite cheerful. "You know about Djaffir's soldier? Well, it is all right now. He is dead!"

"All right!" said I, amazed, for it seemed to me to be rapidly getting worse. "Surely some sort of an inquiry will be made?" "Oh, no! You see it is like this. This soldier, he was not a man from these parts; he came from a long way off—from Asia Minor or somewhere. He has no friends here to ask questions or to avenge him. Probably his family will never know when or where he died. But Djaffir has many friends. They would not like anything to be done to him. Besides, many Turkish soldiers die every year one more or less makes no difference. The man is dead. What use to make a fuss?"

And this was the end. I wished to ask Djaffir how many others he had assisted out of the world just in the ordinary course of events, but I was told this would hurt his feelings, which, it appears, were rather sensitive.

So the unknown soldier went to his unknown grave, and we went our respective ways, I with a feeling that, had the victim been a Christian instead of a mere Moslem, his death would have been "an atrocity" with which to swell consular reports.

The moral of it all is, I fancy, that it is not only the

Christian part of the population that would be the better for a change a government.

But, after all, everything depends upon the point of view.

[from: *Pall Mall Gazette*, London, August 10, 1904.]

Balkan Sketches: Life Is Cheap

It is not very difficult to obtain a *teskereh* (permission to travel in the interior), to hire a horse, and to ride about Turkish territory for a few weeks and see rocks and stones and trees and houses and human beings. It is not even very difficult to get inside the houses as guest, for the Balkan peoples are the most hospitable in all the world. But to get inside the minds of the people is quite another thing. You may travel alone and drop for the time being every Western habit; you may eat with the natives, drink with them, sleep with them, ride with them, live as they do, and watch them patiently for months. You may visit and re-visit their lands and think that you are beginning to understand them. Then a trivial incident, a few words carelessly spoken, or an anecdote told *a propos* of another subject will turn a sudden searchlight upon them, and you perceive, in a flash, that you are as far as ever from seeing things from their point of view. Then it is revealed to you that, to do so, you must leap back across the centuries, you must skip at least six generations of ancestors, you must wipe the West and all its ideas from out you, and let loose all that is left in you of primitive man. Also you must learn six languages all quite useless in other parts of the world.

When you have succeeded in doing all this, you may perhaps be able really to understand and explain the Balkan peoples, and not before. And even then it is only "perhaps."

The difficulty, I may say the impossibility, of this task is probably the reason why, up till the present, all intervention by Western Powers, however well intentioned, has but further complicated the entangled skein of Balkan politics, and, by loosening one knot, has generally succeeded only in tightening all the others.

The flash of the revelation dies away, but afterwards the face of the land is changed. You cannot see it with Eastern eyes. You no longer see it with Western. You are dimly aware that folk at home would be shocked did they know of the ideas that are surging through your mind. You are also aware that the company with whom you are squatting round a wood fire would be equally shocked by your inability to go as far as they go. You are, in fact, in great danger of finding yourself in the unpleasant position of the man of whom it was said, "Hit him hard! he ain't got no friends." And the little flash-light incidents are sometimes so far removed from all Western ideas and experiences—though they possibly may take place only five days' journey from London—that it is almost waste of time to talk to the West about them, for the West imagines it knows better, and flatly refuses to believe them. It either does this, or the truth of the tale is proved beyond all doubt and then the West is so immeasurably shocked that it becomes hysterical and blubbers, as, for instance, it did over Alexander and Draga. For it has a short memory and has quite forgotten the thing that it did only a few generations back when it, too, was young; and it goes on trying to arrange the Balkans on Western Hues—striving, that is, like the Old Man in "Alice." to—

> . . . *madly squeeze a right hand foot*
> *Into a left hand shoe.*

The same things look very different in the East and in the West. The West, for instance was once told that some decapitated heads had been seen on the Bosnian frontier. It recoiled with horror. A large portion of it refused to believe the gentleman who said that he had seen them, and it divided into two parties that screamed at one another, and each took an entirely false view of the situation. But I once heard a very charming Balkan gentleman, while talking about the political situation and the last war (1876-78), mention, by the way, that he had seen little boys sticking cigarettes, or sham ones, in the mouths of severed heads. He added (for he wore European clothing, and spoke a Western language) that such things really ought not to be allowed, but he could not help laughing at the recollection. For he could see, also, the joke, where the West could see only the horror. The West does not remember how short a time has passed since it carried the heads of its own fellow-countrymen on pikes and stuck their quarters about the town. And these are some of the things it should recollect, for, in spite of them, it has evolved a civilisation which it now admires so much that it wishes to force it upon all the world.

The Balkans do not consider this civilisation by any means so perfect. I know many men who would see nothing particularly shocking in a severed head, provided, of course, that it were that of an enemy, but they would never fall so low as to give bad money or wrong change, and their promises are sacred. They maintain that the Western habit of forming bogus companies by which widows and orphans are robbed of their little all is far more reprehensible than occasional brigandage. "Our brigands," they will tell you in Albania, "are poor, very poor men. By working hard they can barely wring a living from the ground. They are quite ignorant; they have never been to any school. They rob to live, and they do so at the risk of their lives. But your brigands have often been to a university, and they rob to obtain luxuries. You have had all the advantages of civilisation and education for years, and this is what you do. But you call us savage because we shoot people."

"I believe a man's life is only worth one cartridge here," I said one day when looking at an Albanian's rifle.

"It isn't always valued so highly," he said. "When taking out the empty cartridge-case, the shooter will sometimes even regret having wasted it on such a worthless object."

The idea amused him. Life is cheap—too cheap—in the Balkans. I could not go so far as he did; but I had been long enough in the land to realise that the Western price set upon the same article is often as ridiculously untrue, and to doubt whether the results of our own systems quite warrant our recommending them wholesale to all who have not yet adopted them.

"You think in England that you are civilised, and that you can teach us," said an Albanian, passionately. "I tell you that there is not an Albanian that would commit crimes such as are to be found in London. There you can find men who will live by selling a woman's honour. This has been printed in your own newspapers. You have had to make a law about it. How do you punish such a man? You put him; in prison and make him pay money! You let such a man live. A man who is a disgrace to all humanity. Bah, we would shoot him like a mad dog! The honour of our women is safe. And you call yourselves civilised."

And it all depends upon the point of view.

[from: *Pall Mall Gazette*, London, September 10, 1904.]

As Others See It:
A Sketch in Old Servia

We sat in the Archimandrite's little room, high up in the big, white-washed monastery: the Archimandrite, dark, dignified, keen-eyed, in long black robe and crimson sash, with a gold cross on his breast; the Montenegrin schoolmaster, a tall Vassoievich man from the Bloody Frontier; the Montenegrin merchant, hook-nosed, with clear grey eyes, travelled and much experienced in things Balkan; the Servian schoolmaster; my Montenegrin guide, Marko, gay in his crimson and blue national costume,—and myself, the only non-Slavonic member of the party. Nature has ordained that betwixt the various human races there should be gulfs that cannot be fathomed and chasms that cannot be bridged; but there is one universal law that holds good everywhere. It is always polite to offer and accept drinks. We drank to one another's good health in beer or cognac according to taste, and as we were on Turkish territory, black coffee was inevitable.

Below, in the courtyard round the white church, surged a dense and parti-coloured crowd of peasants,—folk from Bosnia, the Herzegovina, Montenegro, Servia—men, women and children, gorgeous in gala dress; gold embroidery, silver breast-plates, coin necklaces, peacocks' feathers, bizarre and gaudy artificial flowers, made at home from snippets of Berlin wool and tissue paper, all blazed together in the sunshine. It was Troitzan Dan (Whit-Sunday), when pilgrims flock to the monastery church from all the Servian-speaking lands, and they comprise the larger part of the Balkan Peninsula. The valley rang with national songs and the shrill note of the double pipe. Each sang what pleased him best, regardless of his neighbours, and the effect was more hilarious than musical. Beer and *rakija* flowed freely.

"The nation," said the Archimandrite, "is enjoying itself to-day; but it is the most unfortunate in all Europe."

"That is true," said the Servian schoolmaster emphatically. "There is no nation for whom Europe has so little pity, and no nation to whom she owes more. When the Turk came into the Balkan peninsula, the Serbs were the last to fall. They stood between the Turk and Europe. It was over their bodies that he made his way; when he attacked Vienna, it was the Serb refugees in Hungary that helped Austria to force him back; and of all the conquered peoples, the Serbs, led by Karageorge a hundred years ago, were the first to fight free. Europe owes the Serbs much; they turned back the Turk."

"We were never, never taken," said Marko eagerly. He is a Njegush man, and intensely proud of the fact that of all the Balkan people, the Serbs of Montenegro were never conquered and no Turk ever entered Njegush. "They asked us for poll-tax and maidens for their dirty Pashas, and we gave them powder and shot. And," he went on, turning to the Vassoievich schoolmaster, "you never paid tax either."

The Vassoievich laughed. "Till Europe allowed us to be

Montenegrin after the war of 1876-77 we paid tax to nobody. We were quite wild, as the mountain Albanians are now. There were Turks between us and Montenegro then and we could not join our own people. Unluckily the gentlemen diplomatists of Berlin knew nothing at all about us; they cut our land in half; half the clan they freed, and the rest they handed over to the Turks. Now they wonder that there is always trouble on that frontier. The lot of our brothers under the Turk is harder than before, and we are forbidden to help them. Europe would say Montenegro was causing trouble in the Balkans and would intervene. They are disarmed and helpless."

"She knows," said Marko, "she has been there."

I remembered very vividly the blank misery of that most unhappy corner of all the Sultan's European lands. People in England talk much about Macedonia, but the state of Macedonia is blissful compared to that of corners of Old Servia.

"It is just two years ago since I was there," said I. "How is it now, and what about the reform scheme?"

"The reform scheme," replied the Archimandrite snapping his fingers, "isn't worth—that. Things were bad enough before; they are worse now. Extra money has to be raised to pay these fine foreign officers, and the taxes were already high. You were in Macedonia last year,"—he looked at me sharply, "I wonder if you know what these officers do."

"I was told," I answered cautiously, "that they ate and drank in their quarters and did not trouble themselves otherwise. Of one I heard that he knew no Balkan language and had no dragoman. Certainly the state of the country is no better."

"Of course it isn't," said the schoolmaster, "it was never intended to be."

"The plain truth is," said the merchant, "Russia wants Constantinople and Austria Salonika; neither wishes peace in the Balkans. Europe looks on while they intrigue one against the other, and the Serb people suffer martyrdom. That is the whole story. Now comes this terrible news about the Russian fleet. If it be true, as I fear, Russia can do nothing here. Austria thinks it is her chance. Here, where we are now, the land, though the population is entirely Serb, is recognised by Europe as Turkish, but Austria is on the doorstep with her army. She works night and day to excite a Moslem attack on the Serb Christians, works quietly and silently, and smuggles weapons in pieces into the country to arm the Moslems against us. That is how Austria works reform. When the rising begins, Austria hopes for Europe's permission to march in and quiet it. When Europe says, 'Pray walk in, gentlemen,' the Turk will not dare raise a finger, and Austria will be several days' march nearer Salonika. That is the sort of reform we are taxed for."

"The wrath of God," said the Archimandrite, "has fallen upon Russia. She has forgotten her brother Slavs, and has gone out to heathen lands where she had no business. A curse has fallen upon her. That is my opinion."

"Russia," said the merchant bitterly, "does not care about her 'brother Slavs'; she only wants Constantinople. Servia is not on the road to Constantinople, and she does not trouble about us. And Europe has lied to us and broken faith. In 1877, after five centuries of tyranny, the Turk was crushed. The Serb people hoped to be free at last. Of all, the Herzegovina's had fought most gallantly: they were heroes, the Herzegovina's, and they had won freedom; but Europe gave them to Austria,— to Austria, of all countries! What business has Austria in the

Balkans at all? A small, a very small part of the land only was freed, and is now Montenegrin. Europe said that Austria would arrange and set right the land for a few years only, for twenty-five years. It was hateful to the people, and they would not lay down their arms at first; but they believed that Europe would keep faith with them, and they were persuaded to do so in a luckless hour. Austria has filled her pockets well."

"Had they known," cried Marko, "that it was a lie, the Herzegovinians would have all died fighting on the mountains before they gave up a single weapon."

"The twenty-five years are past," said the schoolmaster, "and far from retiring, the Austrians are now preparing to advance. The fight last week near Bielopolje was incited by them, and meant for a beginning."

The said fight was an attack upon the Serb peasantry by Moslems, in which sixteen Christian Serbs were killed and two women carried off. The forcible abduction of Christian women is only too common in this unhappy district. The Serbs avenged themselves by firing a Moslem village, and the Moslems retorted by burning a Christian one. The rising, which looked ominous, was subdued by Nizams sent hastily to the spot. A very small spark will suffice to fire the Balkans, and the excitement was wild. In the Montenegrin village where I happened to be at the time, news came flying that the Turks were over the frontier and war inevitable. We mobilised the local force with a swiftness that was a sight to see, had our men on the border within six hours of the alarm, telegraphed for a doctor in case of casualties,—and prayed that the news was true and that the Turks would open the ball; but they did not.

"And you believe," I asked the company, "that this rising

was incited by Austria?"

"We are quite certain of it," they replied.

Marko's ideas run principally on deeds of daring, and he values a man entirely according to his thews and sinews. "I don't believe the Austrian army is worth much," he said valiantly; "I don't believe it could fight the Turks. Look at the officers. What is the use of a man who goes into battle with a skinful of beer in front of him? It is a disgrace to a man to stick out in front like that. The Turks are beasts, but they are all thin and hard."

"Austria doesn't fight," said the Archimandrite. "She was well beaten by Italy and Germany. She doesn't fight now; she gets all she wants by plotting and scheming; she never tells the truth and Europe believes all she says. The land swarms with Austrian spies."

"So far as I have seen myself," said I, "Russia is trying to buy one half the Balkan peninsula and Austria the other. I observed a pretty definite line last year dividing the spheres they each work in."

"And that is the truth," said the merchant.

"Thank God," added the schoolmaster, "we have now in Servia a good King with a Servian heart! Had Alexander lived three more years, Servia would have been Austrian. He was a traitor; from the moment he married the woman Draga he was lost; all Servia was in her hands, and she would sell anything and everything."

"But for the Serb people it was a misfortune," I ventured to say, "that Alexander and Draga died in the way they did. It put all Serbs in a bad position in the eyes of Europe." I did not expect anyone to agree with me, but I wanted to hear what they would say. I have haunted Serb lands now for some time, and having been all through Servia just a year before Alexander's fall, had heard and seen enough to understand the nation's attitude. The reply came quickly, "It would have been even worse for Servia, had they lived. It was hideous, if you please, but it was necessary. Desperate diseases need strong remedies. It will be many years before Servia recovers from the Obrenovitch rule. Why cannot Europe understand? The court was a disgrace to all Europe. Do you know what sort of a woman Draga was?"

" Yes, yes," I replied hastily, for the Balkan man when excited is apt to call a spade something more than a spade, and I had already had a sufficiency of unpleasing anecdotes forced upon me.

"For the sake of peace and to save a revolution," said the schoolmaster, "Servia bore much; but it would not be sold to Austria by a bad woman. Make them understand that in England. Austria planned for years and years and almost succeeded; but not quite, thank God! Tell that in England. Now Austria is furious; the plans of twenty-five years have failed; the Serb nation is entirely with King Peter; there was no revolution, as Austria hoped. Why will not England recognise our King that we have chosen, and help us against Austria? The King's position is very difficult. Austria works perpetually to spread falsehoods against him, and she will never cease doing so. The latest thing is that a newspaper, financed by Austria and printed in Austria, has tried to create a quarrel between the two free Servian lands, Montenegro and Servia, by circulating libels about Prince Nikola. Thank God, Prince Nikola has brains! The lies have been entirely disproved, and the plot has failed. The bitter thing to us, who are patriots, is that these tales get into European papers and are believed. Look at the land where we are now. Everyone, whether Christian or Moslem speaks Serb only and is of Serb blood. If this piece of land between Servia and Montenegro could only be given to us and set free, and Servia and Montenegro made one, it would be our salvation. Servia could export its goods freely, for Montenegro has a coast and ports. But Austria will not allow this; she wishes to strangle Servia. Now almost all Servian trade must go through Austria and pay,—pay so heavily—it is death to Servia. But hard as is our position, it is better now than it was. We have a King with a Servian heart, and we can hope."

I have met those who regretted the manner of Alexander's end, but never one who regarded it as other than an event necessary for the nation's salvation, a casting out of abominations. And the crude pictures of Draga's last minutes that adorn the cottages and are inscribed, 'Where would Servia be if this Sodom and Gomorrah had been allowed to continue?' sufficiently indicate the popular point of view. Things look so different in different lights.

"They say now," said the schoolmaster, "that a great Bulgarian propaganda is being worked in England. It will be a terrible misfortune for all the Balkan Slavs if England believes the tales of charlatans, and supports one Slav race for the destruction of the other."

"To me," said I, "it seems a great misfortune that Servia and Bulgaria cannot work together."

"It is a very great misfortune. Bulgarian chauvinism is ruining everything. Bulgaria claims all and each. A huge amount of money is spent on the propaganda."

" I know," said I. "Who pays?"

"God knows! But this is true. Bulgaria now is trying

to work a Bulgar propaganda in Old Servia,—Old Servia, the heart of the Serb nation! This is too much. Montenegro schoolmasters, who are known to be good teachers, have been offered good pay to turn Bulgar and work the propaganda in the Serb schools here. Fortunately they are good patriots and have refused to sell their nation. Bulgaria buys bishoprics of the Turks, and the bishops work only politics."

This I knew from experience to be true. I told how his Grace the Bishop of Ochrida would not even send a priest to the funeral of an unfortunate orphan whose parents had died in the late insurrection, until assured that I would pay.

"Just like the Bulgarian Church," was the comment " Everyone knows that man, and the one at Istih is as bad."

"The Slav people of Macedonia," said the Archimandrite, "are in truth neither Serb nor Bulgar. The two races meet there and the dialect are mixed. What did you think they were?"

"When a British Consul asked me that question," said I, "I replied that if I had £50,000 a year and were free to act, most of them would soon be English."

"And by God you answered truly!" said the merchant. "These poor people only want to be freed from the Turk; anyone can buy them who has enough money. Serb and Bulgar ought to work together to free them. The violent anti-Serb propaganda, worked by Bulgaria, weakens the whole position and prevents the liberation of the land, Ferdinand of Bulgaria wants to be king of wide lands; he cares nothing at all about the Slav race; he is ready to give Servia to Austria in order to gain his own ends; he is a *Schwab* [a contemptuous term for a German] and they are all alike, sly like cats; they plot and crawl in the dark when no one sees. Ferdinand is a fool. He would ruin the Slav people for his own advantage; but if he thinks he will reign in Constantinople, he is much mistaken. He never will; he exists so long as Russia wishes; when Russia gives the word,—good-bye, Ferdinand! There will never be peace in the Balkans till a disinterested nation, that does not want territory, intervenes, Austria, Russia, and Italy only incite the people one against the other for their own purposes. The Turk must go, and the Balkans belong to the Balkan people."

"The Turk also assists in exciting racial differences," I suggested.

"No, not now: he used to; but it is all now done by the Reforming Powers. The Turk knows very well that another general war would be fatal to him. He would be only too glad to have the land quiet; but he is quite powerless. He cannot learn; he never has learned. He cannot reform; he never has reformed. Things now are entirely beyond his control. A Turk is always a Turk; you can do nothing with him except send him back to Asia. You can send him to school, to London, or Paris, or Vienna,—I have known so many, so very many; they came back apparently civilised and with liberal ideas, but in six months they were more Turkish than the rest. Everything European was washed off, as is paint off a woman's face in a rainstorm."

"The Moslems here," said the Vassoievich man, turning to me and laughing, "are greatly excited about you. They do not believe you are a woman. In the bazar this morning there was a report that you were either a Russian consul, or the son of Prince Nikola of Montenegro, in disguise."

"That's the fault of that cursed gendarme who came with us from the frontier," cried Marko. "He brought us by the hell of a track. The Gospodjitza's horse fell in a mud-hole. She jumped off at once and snatched the saddle-bags to save her things from the wet, and the pig of a gendarme, instead of going to help get the horse up, stood there and cried, 'That's a man, I swear!' But the Turks dare not do anything to her; they are afraid of the British fleet. It is extraordinary! By God, I never knew what a great Power England was till I saw her drinking coffee with the Pasha himself, and he as polite as you please!"

Marko, till he saw this wondrous sight, had thought of Pashas only as cutters off of heads and abductors of Christian women, and he has not even yet recovered from his amazement.

As for the Pasha, a grey-bearded diplomatist, he hailed me with as much enthusiasm as did the Serbs; for he too had a point of view which he wished explained in England and he also wanted information.

"It is a great pleasure," he said in excellent French, "to welcome an English lady here. I am a good Ottoman, and England has always been our friend in difficulty. Here, Mademoiselle, I am in a very difficult position; you can scarcely realise how difficult; but I try to do my duty. The land is, as of course you know, Turkish; this was decided by the Berlin Conference; but here are the Austrians on the very doorstep, indeed inside the house. We of course govern, but their soldiers are here, there, everywhere. And, Mademoiselle, they are not yet satisfied; they are trying to advance."

"Are they indeed?" said I.

"Yes, Mademoiselle, I assure you. Oh what a position is mine! On one side the Servians, always plotting against us; on the other side the savage Montenegrins; on the third side the Austrians. I assure you it is very difficult for me."

"I can well believe it," said I.

"England however has always been our friend. I trust she will see justice done. Mademoiselle," he continued sweetly, "you have come through Montenegro. I should very much like to know what there is in Montenegro now."

"Stones and mountains, your Excellency," said I.

"Yes," said the Pasha with an expressive wave of the hand, " that I know, Mademoiselle. But—what are the Montenegrins doing just now?"

"Cultivating the land and taking their sheep to the mountains, Excellency."

"And—er—er—you find it a quiet land to travel in?"

"Perfectly," said I. "No gendarmes are required there." And the subject dropped.

Nor were the Serbs and the Pasha the only ones who had a point of view. Austria, too, was exercised as to the functions of a British subject in a district ear-marked as Austrian in future. The consul hastened to call; so did a decorative officer in a uniform that dazzled Marko. They were both extremely affable, and inquisitive. It surprised them, they said, that an Englishwoman should travel among the Serbs; they had not been aware England took any interest in such people. They made minute enquiries as to the extent of my wanderings. The consul had travelled pretty extensively; that is to say he had explored the greater part of "the Austrian sphere," most Austrian consuls in the Balkans have. I had however out-travelled him; he would much like particulars. I recommended him strongly to go and see for himself those most interesting places. He and the officer both said they were glad I had come, because now I could tell England how *very* much better the land was when regulated by Austria. They were much puzzled, however, as to the reason of my travels. "It cannot be for pleasure," said the consul; "the life is most frightfully hard, as I know."

"Why do *you* travel then?" said I.

"Oh," said the consul, "I am very fond of travelling."

"And so am I," I replied.

Nor did either of us extract much information from the other. Both officer and consul, however, assured me of the great affection Austria bears to Great Britain, and how the nations of the world admire England's sense of justice; and repeating that my visit had afforded them great satisfaction, because I could report truly the state of affairs, they took their leave.

Thus did the oldest inhabitant the Serb, the conqueror the Turk, and the man who would fain succeed him the Austrian, tell their tales to a wandering Briton. And I said to myself: "Truly Marko is right; England is still a very important place." And, in accordance with the request of all three, I report their conversation. But I put the Serb first, for it appears to me that the right is on his side.

Montenegro, July, 1905.
[from: *Macmillan's Magazine - School Guardian*, Edinburgh, November 18, 1905, p. 35-44.]

East and West: A Study in Progress

There is a steamboat on the Lake of Scutari. There ought not to be, I am aware. It is an anachronism—a blot. Other lands have developed slowly—bit by bit—making one step sure before the next advance. The Near East, on the other hand, has been hurled from the Early Middle Ages into the twentieth century, hurled suddenly and pitilessly. She is still giddy and reeling from the shock.

The long flat-bottomed black canoe with a pointed nose, and the yet more primitive "dug-out" were all that the Lake of Scutari had evolved when the steamboat came from the outer world. And as it is with the tangible, visible things, so is it with the inward and invisible ones. The outward signs of the West are forced upon the Near East, but her soul remains "dug-out" and "flat-bottomed with a pointed nose"—primitive, childish, un-evolved.

The steamboat upon which I found myself was a new one—second-hand, of course, but that is new enough in the Near East. It was fairly tidy and moderately clean, and made a brave attempt to keep up a first-class cabin. But I knew its predecessor, and had watched it go from bad to worse, as the blight of the Near East fell on it—till the third-class pervaded it entirely; its uncleaned, unoiled engines squeaked and groaned; its brass rusted into green streaks; its paint blistered, curled, and dropped; and it grew grubbier and yet more grubby. And I did not look forward so hopefully to the fate of the "new" steamer as did its captain—who was also "new"—to the Lake of Scutari.

It was a perfect day. Lake, land, and sky were brilliant with the clean, pure sunshine of early spring. The waters were emerald green, and delicate blue cloud-shadows played over the ghostly ash-grey mountains, whose summits gleamed white with snow. Scutari of the Albanians lay at the lake's foot in a mauve haze. All was gay on board, for it was Easter Monday of the orthodox, and folk—in their very best clothes—were off to visit their relations. The steamboat and I were the only anachronisms. But I did my best to be sociable by going third-class, as did everybody else, and we ate red Easter eggs together. It was a mixed company of Albanians and Montenegrins. Some knew me personally, and some did not. But one does not require introductions in the New East.

"Practical, very practical!" said a Montenegrin, examining with interest my rain-proof, thorn-proof skirt. "It if rains she will not get wet. It if is dirty—no matter! Naturally, of course, one would put on one's best clothes for a journey that everyone may see them. Truly the English are a practical people!" He was resplendent in full dress, and made a brave show. His breast glittered with gold embroidery, he was girt with a silken sash, and he tenderly guarded the full skirt of his white cloth coat from the tarry cordage that lay about.

His son—a slight fair boy, who was not full-grown and

whose moustache was, as yet, almost invisible—was even more gorgeous in what was, in fact, his wedding dress. He was just nineteen and looked as though he ought to be still at school, but was going with his sixteen-year-old bride to visit her parents. They had been already some months married, but were an absurdly childish couple.

We were talking together—I knew friends of his—when another youth approached, a handsome stripling of perhaps one- or two-and-twenty. I did not ask his age, though he would no doubt have willingly told me, for it is a proper question to ask in the Near East. When the Near East "wants to know" there are few, if any, personal details at which it draws the line, and it is equally communicative in return.

My new acquaintance plunged boldly into execrable French and stuck to it bravely, even when I replied in his native language. "But no," he said airily, "I prefer French. *C'est plus chic*. I, you see, Mamzelle, am a man of the world. For example, allow me to present Mamzelle with my card." He searched in the red leather pouch which was girthed under his striped silk sash, and served to hold his revolver and other necessaries—and with evident pride produced a visiting-card with his name in large capitals. "There are few in Montenegro who can give a card like this. Naturally, it was printed abroad!"

I gave mine in exchange, and he continued: "I have travelled. Mamzelle observes that I do not wear my cap at the back of my head like the others. But forward, like this—" he cocked it jauntily. "*C'est plus chic, ça!* There are Montenegrins, of course, who have never been out of this land. *Les pauvres diables*—they know nothing. Now I have passed two years in Florence. I have also," he added with pride, "been in Paris. I know what is *comme il faut*. Why do you wear your hair cut short?" he asked suddenly. "Did you cut it off to make this journey–or why?" I kept my countenance, and replied suitably.

"Mamzelle, then, is not coquette? One sees that, nevertheless, the English possess many admirable qualities," he added reassuringly. "*Attendez!* Since I have travelled I do not admire the women of my own country at all. Decidedly I shall take a wife from abroad."

"Monsieur, I perceive, is not at all patriotic," I said.

He was hurt. "*Mais comment!* Not patriotic. Ah, Mamzelle, it is not so–*parole d'honneur*. But Mamzelle must have remarked how inferior are the women of this country–they are not intelligent, they are not at all *chic*. Whereas the men"–here he expanded his crimson and gold chest and gave a twist to his black moustache–"the men," he continued softly, "are generally admitted to be a truly fine type!"

"Really?" said I.

"But yes, Mamzelle! Surely you admire the Montenegrin type?" he pleaded.

I considered him carefully. "H'm! *assez bien*," said I; "*assez bien*, truly, but indeed I like the women better."

"What, Mamzelle, *assez bien!* Only *assez bien!* But the type is magnificent!"–his horror was such that I remembered the fate of Orpheus–"and you admire the women. But it is impossible. Ah, I understand"–with a sudden flash of inspiration–"you are brave, you travel alone, you have short hair, you admire the women; you are perhaps a man dressed up! A woman," he added profoundly, "never admires women."

"Monsieur is talking nonsense," said I. I referred him to various of the high and mighty of the land, including the Prime

Minister. The exalted nature of my acquaintances had a very marked effect on him, and he hastily withdrew the charge. "Also," he added, "I remark –" here he entered upon personal and anatomical details which it is unnecessary to particularise, and was so convinced that he was making himself agreeable that it was hard to preserve the severe gravity the occasion demanded.

"Then if it is really true that Mamzelle admires more the women than the men, she will perhaps give a reason."

"Certainly," said I. "I admire the women because they are much more industrious and often work hard. The men, I find, ordinarily do not work much, but smoke and drink coffee. That I do not admire! I think that they should work too."

He might, and indeed *ought* to have replied: "They toil not, neither do they spin. But behold, Solomon in all his glory was not arrayed like one of these!" But he did not. He was horrified.

"What, Mamzelle, that the women should not work, but that the men should! *Mais, mon Dieu! mon Dieu!* Then if you married you would expect that your husband should work?"

"Certainly, I should make him!"

"Then," said he scathingly, "I will never, never marry an Englishwoman. Never, never. Mamzelle; you understand." This was evidently meant to be a cruel blow and to shatter all my hopes. "Monsieur is quite right," I answered cheerfully. "With an English wife he would not be happy. He should take a nice young girl of his own country."

"And I shall marry, soon–very soon. I have not the stupid idea of the English, to wait till they are quite old – thirty, perhaps–before marrying. It is much better like Marco there"–he indicated the bridegroom–"his clothes suit him marvellously," he added reflectively.

I thought the subject of marriage was now thrashed out. But no. When the Near East "wants to know" it is extraordinarily persistent. He was of a forgiving nature.

"I like to talk to the ladies," he said, "even when they are cruel." Here he bowed gallantly. "You have many acquaintances in Montenegro. I believe that you must already have given your heart to one of them. *Car enfin*–the type is truly magnificent. Mamzelle assuredly is not made of stone."

The question worried him much, and produced much fruitless discussion. We were rapidly approaching his destination, and it was still unsolved. The flat-bottomed black canoes were putting out from the shore. He called the steward boy and demanded a bottle of beer. Knocking off the top casually he pressed me to take a glass. "You understand this is a great compliment that I make you!" I drank his health tepid foam. "If you really do not want any more I will finish it myself," he said; and he did so. "*Au revoir bientôt*, Mamzelle!"

He descended into the clumsy canoe with a dangerously large crowd of others, and as it wobbled shorewards it struck me as a good subject for a snap-shot. I hastened astern to catch it as it passed. He perceived the camera, and a radiant smile spread over his countenance. "*Le type monténégrin*" had evidently impressed me to such a degree that I was anxious to obtain his portrait. And as the crazy craft waggled away among the willows at the river's mouth he stood up and waved enthusiastically.

The ambition of his rude forefathers was to be reckoned mighty warriors and to die fighting for the fatherland. The desire of his soul was to be thought "*très chic*."

The past is gone beyond recall. The new world is not yet formed. The child-people remain–disorganised, demoralised, their mental health destroyed by a heavy diet of new ideas which they are totally unable to digest.

The Near East is a land of sorrow and of much suffering. Its worst enemies to-day are those who wish to hustle it too quickly into what is called "civilisation."

[from: *The Westminster Gazette*, 14 September 1908.]

Albanian and Montenegrin Folklore

Symbolic extinction of household fire.— In Montenegro, when the last male of a family was shot, it was customary for the chief woman of the house to throw water on the hearth and extinguish the fire as a symbol of the extinction of the family. The custom is not yet extinct among the peasants when the last male of a family dies.

Communal justice.— There has been recently (about February, 1912) an extraordinary case of rude justice in the Fandi bariak of Mirdita. A certain family has long been a pest to its neighbours, robbing, shooting, and being generally objectionable. The local heads held a sitting and condemned the whole of the males of the family to death. Men were told off to ascertain the whereabouts of the various victims, and pick them off. On the appointed day the whole seventeen males were shot. Of them one was only five, and another twelve years old. To any protest against the brutality of killing a child in cold blood, the reply is,— "It was bad blood, and must not be propagated!" It seems incredible, but I was assured that it was actually intended to shoot a wretched woman because she was *enceinte,* and might bear a male who would continue the inherited evil. Three shots, which missed, were fired at her. She then rushed to a man and called on him to protect her, and he took her in *besa* (a peace oath), and she was spared.

Mourning custom.— It is perhaps noteworthy that, whereas in Montenegro face-scratching as a sign of mourning is done by *women,* in North Albania it is only done by *men,* and it is not proper for women to do it. I was at a funeral at Skreli before Christmas, and all the men had already clawed their temples, which were red and inflamed with scratches; no women were clawed.

Divination.— It is of interest just now to note what attention is being paid to the signs on bladebones and fowl breastbones. They are read eagerly, and, I am earnestly assured, foretell nothing but blood.

Folk-medicine.— I was recently down on the plains of Bregu Mati distributing quinine to the luckless people who were penned on the plains by the troops throughout last fever season. I found a great many very bad cases of enlarged spleen. The local remedy for this is to take a sheep's spleen, lay it over the seat of disease, and then hang it by the fire and roast it all away, when the disease will disappear with it.

If you see a snake swallowing a frog, this is a most valuable opportunity to obtain a cure for epilepsy. You must throw a handkerchief, preferably a black one, over the snake. In its fright it will disgorge the frog. Keep the handkerchief and, when any one falls down in a fit, throw it over the patient's head. The patient will then likewise disgorge the disease.

I am myself becoming the centre of a myth, and am supposed to have wrought a cure on a man I never touched. He was shot in the head during last year's revolution, and his recovery is entirely ascribed to me, and not to the doctor to whom it was due.

Taboos at childbirth.— In Montenegro, though a woman is expected, among the peasants, to be fit to carry wood and water three days after childbirth, she is not allowed to cook and make bread until she has been "churched." I learnt this while living in a peasant house at Njegush, through commenting with horror on the case of a young married woman who, by carrying wood too early, brought on her death. I was told that fetching wood was quite a right and proper thing for her to do, but that, *of course,* she would not be allowed to make bread or cook. When I asked "Why?" I was told that bread so made could not possibly be eaten; it was not right; it was never done;—and so forth. All the company agreed on this point.

I have recently learnt also that in Montenegro it is regarded as impossible for childbirth to be allowed at the house of the mother's parents. Should such a thing be permitted, it would bring the worst luck,—nay, absolute ruin,—on her brothers, who, of course, live in the parental home. I know of a case even among the upper and educated class. A young married lady went to visit her mother, and had to shorten her stay for the above reason. Her grandmother nearly drove her out of the house, and said on her departure,—"Thank God! You have gone, and haven't brought evil on the house!"

I have been making enquiries on the subject here in Scutari. I find that a mother is not allowed to visit a married daughter till after the birth of her first child. I enquired if under any circumstances the daughter could go to her mother's for such an event, but this seemed quite a new idea. People did not definitely say that it was impossible, but they did not seem to imagine that any such necessity could ever occur. The mother is not allowed to attend at the birth of her daughter's child, at any rate never the first time. Later on it appears not to matter so much,—but there was uncertainty, and I gather that it is not done. Should no child be borne after a year of marriage, the prohibition of the mother's visit is removed?

It is customary to break an egg over the face of a newborn child. Therefore eggs are a correct present to take to a house after the occurrence of a birth. The breaking of the egg is, so far as I can make out, to avert the Evil Eye.

Foundation sacrifices.— Cocks and lambs are still often sacrificed when foundations of houses are laid in North Albania. The citadel at Scutari is one of the many buildings of which it is told that a human being was built into the foundations. This particular event, according to an old and powerfully dramatic ballad, occurred early in the fourteenth century, when this place was under Serb rule. Devils destroyed by night what was built by day, and only after sacrificing the young wife of one of the three young Princes could the building be reared. The tradition of such burials in foundations has survived till recent years. An Austrian engineer in Bosnia told me in 1906 that some twelve years previously, a panic was caused by a report that the Austrians were going to brick a child into the foundations of a bridge. This bridge was being built over the Lim, and, owing to the incapacity of the engineer, was so badly constructed that it fell twice. When the third attempt to erect it was made, the people took fright, and were only with difficulty persuaded that no human sacrifice would take place.

Objection to portraits.[i]— The late Mr. Holman Hunt has

---

i cf. *Folk-Lore,* vol. xviii., p. 83 (Vaud).

repeatedly told me that, when he began his painting in Palestine, he had the greatest difficulty in getting people to sit to him as models, owing to a belief that, when the Day of Judgment came, the portrait might arrive first at the Gates of Heaven and be admitted, and the rightful owner of the name be dismissed as an impostor. A month or two ago I met again the aged man who was afraid lest my sketch of him might cause his death, as mentioned in Dr. Frazer's book.[ii] He had not forgotten the episode, and was glad to hear that the sketch was locked up quite safely.

Tabu on names.— I have been for the last seven months engaged in distributing relief (clothing, roofing material, etc.) to the luckless Albanians whose property was entirely destroyed in the disturbances last year. This necessitates keeping a list of the families who have received relief, and it is usually only with great difficulty that a woman can be induced to give her husband's name. She always gives her own maiden name. When pressed as to her husband's name, she very often says,— "Ask that other woman," pointing to a comrade, "she knows." The only reason I can obtain for this is,— "Modesty; of course she is too modest to say to which man she belongs." Even here in Scutari, until very recently, it was never the custom of a (Christian) man and wife to recognise each other in the street, and they very seldom, if ever, went out together. I was given the same reason,— "She would not like people to know he was her husband." The last ten years, however, have seen rapid changes. It was fortunate that I visited the Albanian mountaineers when I did, for that year (1908) was the last in which they were to be seen in their primitive state.

---

ii *The Golden Bough,* (3rd edition), Part ii., *Taboo etc.,* p. 100.

Burial customs.— It is customary in the mountains of Shala and Dushmani, and possibly elsewhere, to leave some iron article in a new-made grave until the corpse is brought for interment. It is unlucky to step over an empty grave.

Bridal customs.— In the Crmnica valley in Montenegro (and possibly in other parts), it was, and among peasants may still be, the duty of the two *djevers* (bride-leaders) who came to fetch the bride to see that no one tied knots in the fringe of her *strukka* (a long straight shawl, worn like a Scottish plaid and with very long fringes at each end). Should some malevolent person succeed in doing this, the bride would either miscarry with her first child or bear a cripple.

Divine right.— It is amazing how greatly the tribesmen believe in "the divine right of kings." The hereditary chief of the Mirdites, Prenk Pasha, was looked on as but little short of a god when he returned from exile in 1908. Now, although after three years' experiences the Mirdites and other tribes are disappointed in him, they still have a superstitious belief in his power. I have frequently been told that "The Mirdites cannot do [so and so], because Prenk will not allow them. They would *like* to of course. But what can they do?" When I have pointed out that one man cannot possibly prevent thirty thousand people taking separate action if they wish, I am always told,— "But he was born chief. He is sent by God. They have to do what he says."

Scutari.
[from: *Folk-Lore: a Quarterly Review of Myth, Tradition, Institution and Custom*, London, 23 (1912), p. 224-229.]

The Soul of the War

To the Editor of 'The Nation'

Sir,—I have just returned from sixteen savage days near the front, in the war-swept land that lies on the shores of Lake Scutari. A land, be it remembered, which has now been at war since April, 1911. For last year's insurrection of the Maltsori was the forerunner of all that is now happening. Poor folk! They hoped to have finished last year—that either war or European intervention would have ensued, but Europe made one final effort to maintain the reign of horror known as "the *status quo.*" And now, for the second year, the Maltsori are on the battlefield.

Last year almost every Christian house was burned and the land devastated by the Turkish army. Now—before it has had time to recover—the Montenegrin army has poured over it and almost every Moslem house is burnt. Four years ago, before the Young Turks began to take active measures to crush Albania; this was a wondrously fair land—fertile, rich in gardens, maize, and tobacco. Now it is a wilderness, strewn with blackened ruins and heaps of ashes, and ploughed up by the wheels of artillery.

Hour after hour I stood on rocky hills listening to the hum of shells, watching the white puffs of smoke that marked where they fell, hearing the death-rattle of the machine guns. War was before me—around me. Its huge, hideous, shapeless body lay on all the land—monstrous and incredible —heaving itself, slowly, ever forward.

And the question that seemed most insistent was: "What is the power that drives it onward? What is the soul of this body?" For even the most deformed possesses a soul.

What can move a people to face—for the second year, not merely with courage but enthusiasm—hunger, cold, wet, fatigue, and perhaps wounds and death? I was with no paid army sent by a government—I was with the men of the Gruda tribe, one of those that revolted last year.

Lean, haggard men, exhausted by nearly two years' struggle, they had left their houses—only partially repaired since last year's burning—again to face the enemy. Death and hardship have sadly thinned the tribe; they frankly said they were sick of war.

What gleam were they following? It was not the tobacco, which they freely looted; it was not merely the thirst for vengeance, though that was strong. It was a belief, firm and fixed, in the righteousness of their cause, the belief that they were fighting for freedom, that after nearly 500 years the power of the Turk was broken, the curse removed.

Of this they were quite convinced. "The Powers," they said, "can never again make us live under the Turk. They can kill us. But make us accept the Turk—never!" Before them they saw the dawn of a new era—a promised land—and they pressed forward, guided by the star of freedom. No sacrifice was too great. Of their dead they said: "Let him die; it is for freedom and the Cross." It was moving and pathetic—for which of us ever finds the promised land? But in all the squalor and horror, it was the one redeeming spot.

We lived together, crowded like wild beasts upon straw, in half-burnt houses. Daily they went out to slaughter, returning with blood upon their feet, to hack with a sword bayonet the sheep roasted whole, which formed almost our sole diet. Rations of bread ran very short. It was a hideous life of blood and muck. And at night they howled barbaric chants of the fights last year against Tourgoud Pasha.

One Moslem was of the party, on quite equal terms with all the others. For he too was a foe of the Turk. For the Moslem who sides with the Turk, they have no pity.

The evicting of the foreign invader and all his friends is their object—"let them all go to Asia!"

It is the uprising of the West against the East—the European against the spirit of Asia. It is also "earth hunger," the desire of a people to possess the land of its forebears. Slowly and for years these feelings have been strengthening. The Powers have vainly tried to crush them. Repression has only made the final explosion more violent. For the bloodshed and misery, the so-called civilised Powers of Europe are wholly responsible. They failed to keep the promises given over thirty years ago. Their conjoint action presents no redeeming feature.

For the one gleam in the present night, we must turn to the wild tribesman who gives all he has for freedom. The misery which must inevitably follow this two years of devastation will be most dire. It will be no promised land that the tribesman will find when peace is made. Let no friend of freedom forget that the first to show Europe that the Turk was not invincible was the North Albanian tribesman. When his hour of need comes—as come it must—may he not be without help! — Yours, &c.,

M. Edith Durham.

[from: *The Nation*, 16 November 1912, p. 310, reprinted in *Living Age*, Vol. 275, December 1914, p. 693-695.]

The Advance Guard of the War

To the Editor of 'The Nation'

Sir,—In the article on the "First Week of the War" that appears in your issue of October 19th are some misconceptions which it would be desirable to correct, as they give an erroneous idea of what took place last year. This war practically began last year. Your correspondent states that the Turks completed the fortifications around Scutari in the summer of last year, and that an inspection of these fortifications by Russian officers led these gentlemen to consider a Montenegrin invasion useless.

The fact is, however, that all these fortifications have been either constructed or completed since the Maltsor insurrection—*i.e.*, during the winter of 1911-12, and especially this spring and summer. So that the Russian officers could not have seen the Turkish fortifications "because they were not yet in sight."

The thing that prevented the outbreak of war last year was the fact that the Turks—in order to quell 1,800 Maltsors—brought about 50,000 troops and placed them in strong positions thickly along the Montenegrin frontier before Montenegro's troops were ready, and before the necessary artillery tracks were completed in Montenegro.

The attack had, therefore, to be postponed. When the Maltsors were commanded to withdraw from Montenegro, it was an understood thing that so soon as the Turkish troops should evacuate the district, these various heights were to be occupied by Maltsors. An advance would then in all probability have been made last winter.

A part, however, only of the Turkish troops left the immediate frontier, and the whole army—or a very large part of it—was sent, in feverish haste, to fortify Scutari and the frontier, both of which were almost unprotected.

Tarabosh fort was not yet completed, and none other existed save the old Venetian citadel. The fortification of Tarabosh was the first "reform" begun by the Young Turks at Scutari. And a road up that mountain, made by forced Christian labor, first showed the Christians the benefits they were likely to receive from "Konstitutzoon."

Brdica and Tepe were only fortified in the spring. The work on Tepe, in fact, I saw commenced. As for the frontier, Vranje (erroneously called Hornu by you) was made into a modern fortress with strong artillery. Ramparts were made on Dechich and guns taken up. Iugi is a mere village and has never itself been fortified. It lies at the foot of Dechich, and depended on that and on Shipchanik—a fortified hill—for protection. Shipchanik is a quite old-fashioned fortification, untenable against modern artillery. Planinitza and Miljosh were also fortified last winter and spring.

In truth, had the Turks spent half the money thus wasted,

on making the roads and schools promised to the Maltsors, things might have turned out differently.

As for the military road by which your correspondent imagines the Montenegrins to be advancing on the side of the lake, that also was one of the Turks' many abortive schemes. A small part only was ever finished, and when I was there, ten days ago, we plunged through mire and water, often knee deep.

As for Scutari, the plain between it and the lake is, to my own knowledge, very strongly fortified. I rode across it last May and found work—going on in hot haste on all sides. And barbed wire was passing through Scutari in cart loads. Two, perhaps three, subterranean bomb-proof forts were being made, and several small wire tangles and ditches. Some Christians with Moslem names succeeded in getting employment in these works and revealed the details.

Such is the tale of Scutari's fortifications.

The Maltsors watched the work with growing anxiety. They knew that they could not afford to let the Turks grow stronger, and hesitated where to turn. They had been severely disappointed last year by Montenegro's failure to support them.

The war with Italy inspired temporary hope that Italy would be the one Power that dared attack Turkey in Europe. This hope failed. But the mere fact that a European Power *had* attacked was inspiring. The year dragged on, spring passed, and Montenegro was still not ready. The Maltsors made a final appeal to Austria, saying the situation was quite intolerable. They were bidden wait another year. This settled the question. They chose Montenegro and attacked upon all the outlying Turkish posts in the mountains. Their first hope had been alliance with the Moslem tribes of Kossovo, and a fight for autonomy. The Moslems, however, suddenly made peace with the Turkish Government without any consideration of—and without consulting—the Christians. These, desperate, then decided to get rid of the Turk at any price, and by expelling all the outlying soldiers from Maltsia-e-madhe, and by descending in force at Kastrati, and cutting off and driving back the reinforcements that started from Scutari, succeeded in isolating Dechich, Tuzi, and its surrounding fortresses, and also in cutting the water canal to Tuzi. The way was thus prepared for the Montenegrins' attack, the result of which I need not repeat.

The Albanian question has not yet been answered, and the last of it will not be heard for many years.

One little remark further I would like to make. In one of your paragraphs you state that I have been going about in "semi-royal state." The truth is that I've shifted for myself entirely; bought and cleaned my own horse, and, when over the frontier, depended for food entirely on the charity of one of the Maltsor tribes. Except for liberty to go at my own risk, I have had no help at all. —Yours, &c.,

M. E. Durham

[from: *The Nation*, 30 November 1912, p. 392-393.]

Miseria

"It isn't an illness," said a little Croatian sister, whose business it is to count the shirts and sheets, and see that the Montenegrin maidens do not steal them from the Montenegrin sick and wounded - for your Montenegrin woman is a rare thief, and will plunder anywhere.

"It is not illness - it is only miseria!"

A human wreck - a fragment left by the wave of war - lay gasping and retching.

"Miseria" Only miseria! It is what we are suffering from here now. "Red Crosses," English, Austrian, French, Italian, Russian, Bohemian, swarm. They struggle indeed for patients. They are fitted up with wondrous surgical appliances - but - they will take no infectious cases. And the aftermath of every war is illness - not wounds. So the beautiful and costly foreign hospitals, which absorb all the best buildings, remain half-empty, and we - who are attached to the Montenegrin Red Cross - wrestle with typhus, enteritis, gastritis, dysentery, and smallpox - all mixed together in one seething mass.

In spite of the fact that a marked and typical case of smallpox was in the ward, the Montenegrin authorities persisted it was chickenpox, and poured in other patients, till too late. And these wretched "other patients"! Patient is indeed the word that fits them. Suffering intolerable and incredible! Miseria!

One lay in a corner on a filthy straw mattress, and stank most sickeningly. There he lay moaning ceaselessly.

"Dysentery - very typical," said the doctor.

"Don't go near him," said a Montenegrin maiden: "he stinks."

In truth, "miseria" summed him up. An elderly man, stricken for a fortnight with acute dysentery - emaciated, hardly human in his filth. His extreme forlornness was appealing.

He muttered feebly, "I've worn these clothes for a month and a half. I cannot live any longer. I can't sleep for the vermin. My foot is dead. They tied it up ten days ago." Such words - feeble and disjointed - told his tale. We loosened the filthy bandage, and the little toe, bone and all, came off with it. Lice rushed from the oozing sore. It was frost-bite. "Ten days and nights," he moaned, "I walked through snow, sometimes up to my breast. Then I was ill. My other leg hurts too!" His other leg was raw and suppurating.

Another frost-bite.

He had been ordered milk by the doctor. But no one had been there to see that he had it, and for two days little but dirty water had passed his lips. Then a Bosnian doctor and his wife, a Russian doctor, and a few other foreign assistants came as volunteer helpers. "If it weren't for the strangers, we should all be dead!" said an unhappy man.

But even with "the strangers," miseria triumphs. A man - all that remained of one - was brought in, moaning horribly. Three days and nights he had lain in a ditch of snow, and, though marble-cold, was still alive. Conscious, alas! and in agony. But he survived only a day in spite of all efforts.

General Vukotich's army plunged through snow for ten days, and slept in it for ten nights, in order to come from "Old Servia" to Scutari. Bronchitis, pneumonia, and rheumatism are the price paid. And, alas! from Turkish territory they carried smallpox.

Here, in the hospital, lie men, whose legs to the knee and above are cold as stone. They cannot sleep for the aching. And not more than one blanket is available to each. Almost all, when they arrived, were stockingless, and not a pair of socks or stockings can Podgoritza produce.

"It isn't the fighting I mind; it is the lying awake all night as cold as ice. If we could only have a bit of fire!" said one. But wood is hard to get, and the stove smokes.

Endless rubbing with camphor and mustard spirit fails to stir more than a feeble and temporary circulation.

An icy wind blows - shrieks - tears the water cans from the hands of the women, who struggle up from the river with them. Bang - crash goes a window-pane, and a blast cuts over the miserable, shivering beings on their filthy mattresses. A gum-pot and a daily paper from England serve as temporary repair.

Fresh glass cannot be obtained, as all workmen are out as soldiers. Service in the hospital is largely performed by Turkish prisoners.

Miseria! If this be the price paid by the conquerors, the woe of the conquered must be untold and incredible.

Scutari - Scutari, the joy of all lovers of the picturesque and beautiful - lies starving and suffering but a day's journey distant. And around it, freezing and shoeless, and suffering, is the besieging army.

Why is it that so much sympathy is expended on the wounded? The wound from a modern rifle - if it does not touch a vital part - is comparatively insignificant.

The speed of the bullet partly cicatrises the wound, and if it be kept even moderately clean, it heals in a fortnight. And the wounded has always a certain glory that buoys him up.

It is the victims of miseria that are truly pitiable. Those that drop in the track and rot.

And miseria is the price of war!

"The Balkan land for the Balkan people." But the Balkan lands were but sparsely populated, and the victims are innumerable.

At the beginning of September, when all was being prepared for war, and the Serb inhabitants of Kosovo vilayet being daily supplied with rifles, a Serb of Plava said, "Last year the Maltsori of Maltsia-e-madhe revolted. They fought fair; they never assaulted a woman, nor burnt a mosque, nor mutilated a body. They hoped Europe would intervene and protect them, and recognise that they had fought as civilised people. What did Europe do? She hurled those people back to the Turks with never a guarantee of any sort. She supported the Turks who burnt, mutilated, and assaulted. This has taught us a lesson. Europe likes horrors. Very well - she shall have them. This war that is just going to begin will surpass all others, We will take eye for eye - head for head. Then perhaps Europe will be satisfied!"

This programme has in truth been carried out. All that the Turk has done for five centuries has been repaid him in one supreme blood-bath.

The vengeance is colossal and complete. But the price paid is Miseria.

"There will be no Moslem problem," says many a Balkan man, "because we have killed them nearly all off. Those that survive will have been taught a lesson they will not forget."

To us on the spot, with "Peace" now almost in sight, the question is, what will be the result of the struggle that must inevitably follow? The struggle against no human foe, but the struggle against the horror that will fall alike upon victor and vanquished as they reel exhausted from the fight – the struggle with Miseria.

M. E Durham

[from: *The Nation*, 21 December 1912, p. 527-528.]

Hil

I

The sun glared fiercely on a dazzling wilderness of rock, that beat back the heat in great waves till all the mountains reeled and whivered in swirls of hot air.

In a shadow like an ink blot, cast by a little crooked oak, sat Hil, crouched on his heels, and stared miserably at a parched patch of earth, whereon rows of half-grown maize were shrivelling, all yellow, in the sun.

Poor little field, hacked by a hoe, scattered with seed and harrowed by a bundle of brushwood weighted with a stone. The weary hours that had gone to the making of it were all in vain. Inch by inch had Hil and his brother pounded holes in the rocks with a crowbar, rammed them with powder, and piled the resultant fragments round in a rude wall. Countless little sackfuls of earth had they collected and carried. And now all hope of bread for the winter was gone.

The heavy blue sky closed down like a lid on the aching land. No cloud brought hope; not a leaf stirred; nor was there any sound save the wailing bleat of five sheep that crowded into the shadow close to Hil, striving to escape the sun's rays.

Man and sheep were scarce distinguishable. Hil's ragged *chakshirs* were of home-spun undyed sheep-wool, and the only garment on his back was a sheepskin coat. The shining row of brass cartridges in his belt was his sole distinction!

The sheep gasped and panted. They had drunk no water since the night before—every well and spring was dry. Hil's sufferings were greater even than theirs. He shook with fever, contracted last time he was on the plains, and he had the added misery of a hopeless future.

It was useless to stare at the maize. He rose to his full height of not much more than five feet; for he was one of the little dark, hill-men whose forefathers fought the Romans, in the days when the land was known as Illyria.

Shifting the long strip of dirty cotton that bound his shaven head, so as the better to protect it from the sun, he crossed from the shadow to his hovel, which, built and roofed with slabs of unhewn rock, merged almost invisibly into the stony wilderness.

'Water!' he said; 'give me water.'

A ragged woman, wearing a stiff bell-shaped skirt woven of black sheep's wool and worked in curious devices, rose wearily, as was her duty when the *zoti i shpis* (house-lord) entered. She tucked her distaff under one arm and went on spinning a coarse wool thread with a dexterous twist of her fingers.

'There isn't any' she said. And as she spoke, she took Hil's Martini, which he unslung as he entered, and hung it to a peg of projecting stone.

'Why isn't there any?'

'I gave it to the child,' she said.

The child, a sickly boy of about nine, lay on a heap of

dry fern in one corner, too listless to drive away the flies that swarmed on his face and filthy rags.

Gjoko was not Hil's son. Hil had inherited his elder brother's widow as wife and adopted his child. Drana had passed from one brother to the other as a matter of custom and convenience. The priest, after vainly protesting, had excommunicated the couple. But the church was an hour distant, up the mountain-side, and tribe-law was more binding on Hil than church-law. Moreover, in no other way could Hil have obtained a wife. For he was a very poor man, and wives, in the mountains, have to be bought with money. And the present comfort of possessing a woman far outweighed the vague possibility of Hell in the future.

He picked up the flat-shaped water-barrel that Drana had carried up before sunrise from the shrunken yellow Drin that flowed in the valley nearly two thousand feet below.

But the little barrel gave forth no answering rattle. He pulled out the maize-cob plug. But no drop flowed.

He sat down heavily on a block of tree-trunk by the side of the hearth-stone, rolled a cigarette, and poked vainly for a spark in the gray heap of wood-ash, over which hung an empty cauldron. Finally, with a flint and steel, from the leathern pouch at his belt, he kindled the cigarette and smoked his very last pinch of tobacco in silence.

Then he said: 'The maize is all dead.'

'I know. Why did you sow it all? Why did you not keep some to eat?' asked Drana, spinning ceaselessly, like one of the Fates.

'How was I to know there would be a drought? We had a good crop enough last year. Perhaps it is because we are excommunicated,' he said.

'It is because of God's will and the sun,' retorted Drana. 'Lulash's maize and Deda's are as bad, and they aren't excommunicated. And the Padre's own well is dry. You aren't going to turn me out?' she asked anxiously. 'Where could I go? and the child?'

'No,' he snapped, 'I shan't turn you out. But you must fetch up more water. I can't start with the charcoal till I've had a drink. God knows how I shall get to Scutari. It is this cursed fever!—I believe there is a curse on us,' he added doubtfully.

'Curse!' cried Drana furiously, 'curse! There's a curse on all the land. It is the accursed Moslems. Since they shot my husband and stole the donkey we've had nothing but misery!'

Hil made no reply. Drana spun. The flies crawled over the comatose child. And the earth turned slowly towards night.

Slowly the sun sank, flooding all the suffering land with splendour. Drin flowed, a river of gold, in a mystic purple valley, and a rosy light flushed all the peaks. The distant church-bell clanked through the still air.

'Aksham,' said Hil. He stood up, and, crossing himself, muttered, '*Ora pro nobis, ora pro nobis—in terra pax—per saecula saeculorum,*' and such other of the mysterious words he had heard in church as he could remember, vaguely hoping by their means to propitiate the Being that had blighted his maize.

Drana, too, crossed herself, thrust the distaff into her wide, nail-studded belt, and then picked up the water-barrel and corded it to her shoulders.

There rose a mingled bleating of goats and sheep and the lowing of cows, as the tribe gathered its flocks together and poured them down the cliff for their one drink in the twenty-four hours. Panting, struggling, sending showers of loose stones bounding into the valley below, the parched beasts leapt and staggered from rock to rock down to the river, plunged in and drank rapturously, greedily, till they were distended water-skins.

It was late, very late, when Drana reached the hovel again, bending under the full water-barrel. The rest of the mountain folk followed even more slowly, for their water-logged beasts were too parched to browse by day—now stopped to pluck at each scrap of withered herbage between the rocks.

With a long whistling sigh of relief, Drana slackened the cords and swung the barrel to the ground. She filled with water a long-handled bowl—made of a bottle-gourd cut lengthwise—and gave drink to the half-unconscious child. Hil picked up the barrel and drank greedily from the bung-hole.

Drana took a heavy slab of unleavened maize-bread from a basket that hung from the rafters, broke it in halves and gave one piece to Hil.

'Is that all?' he asked.

'All till you come back from Scutari,' she replied. 'Wilt have some bread, Gjoko?'

'No,' whined the child.

Drana ate a few mouthfuls and put the rest back in the basket. 'He will be hungry, perhaps, to-morrow,' she said. 'When I go up to the forest to cut wood, I will get some leaves to boil with it. Don't be more than two days away.'

Hil was cording a black sack of charcoal to his shoulders. Drana held it while he tied the knots.

'Sell it at a consulate if you can,' she said, 'and perhaps the servants will give you something to eat. They gave me five lovely onions at the Italian Consulate.'

The sack was made fast. She stooped and picked up a

second. Hil bent and she swung it up on top of the first. It rested against his head and the back of his neck. He steadied it with one hand, took his Martini in the other and stepped a few paces from the door.

'Don't forget the salt!' cried Drana. She had tasted no salt for over a fortnight and craved for it as some for brandy.

Hil stopped. Then stepped a few more paces. Then he staggered and sat down heavily on a rock.

Drana hurried out.

'It's the fever,' he panted. 'I can't carry more than one. It's no use. Take the other back.'

Drana was aghast. 'But one sack won't buy maize for a week,' she said. 'It was three before we lost the donkey, and that was little enough. Then it was two, and now it must be one. If I come too to carry the other, Gjoko will die of thirst—.'

'God is great!' said Hil. 'When I've sold the charcoal I'll carry round the sack and beg bread at house-doors. You must cut a lot of wood to-morrow. Then perhaps next week we'll be able to carry down three lots—God willing!'

He rose with difficulty, balanced the one sack and started again. Staggering down the rocky track, aching with fever and supporting himself from time to time on his Martini, he disappeared into the vast loneliness of the night—one speck of suffering humanity under a myriad pitiless stars.

★ ★ ★

It was long past noon on the second day. But Hil came not. Drana squatted in the hovel, spinning mechanically. Hil, she reckoned, should have arrived at Scutari in ten hours, even allowing for his weak state. He would sell the charcoal for one and four pence, and then, after a sleep, go a-begging with the sack.

Only when he had begged all the food he could, would he spend the precious money. He would tramp back by night. He was overdue.

Gjoko lay moaning. She offered him boiled beech and dandelion leaves—other food there was none—and strove to cheer him with hopes of the onions and salt that perhaps Bab would bring. So the day passed.

The sun sank and the stars rose, but Hil came not. There was but little water left in the barrel she had filled before sunrise. She had no strength to fetch more. The night rolled on. She lay on the earthen floor, stupid with exhaustion, till a great shout tore through the gray dawn:

'Oy Drana Nikia! Oy! Oy!!'

Up the track toiled slowly Lulash and Deda, her nearest neighbours, whose huts were not more than three-quarters of an hour distant, and between them, seated on a rifle, they bore Hil, limp and almost unconscious.

They laid him on the floor.

'Found him half-way. He'd fallen over a rock,' said Lulash, and cast down the charcoal sack, filled with dirty scraps of food, beside him.

II

Five weeks dragged slowly by. Five times did Drana tramp to the town and each time brought back a sack of stale crusts and fragments. Single-handed she could not cut and burn enough charcoal to keep things going. Hil had to sell his only possession of value—his beloved Martini. And on its price they lived till Hil, bruised, sprained and fever-stricken, should again be fit to work.

But to Hil it was like eating his own flesh and blood. For with the Martini he had avenged his brother.

Then a marvel came to pass. Drana came back from Scutari laden not only with food but with news.

'The Turks have gone!' she cried. 'God and St. Nikola be praised. The Turks have gone!' She crossed herself.

'What are you saying, woman?' growled Hil.

'It is true as I believe in God,' she said. 'In Scutari all are shouting and singing "*Liria! Liria*!!" (Freedom!). Ask Lulash if you don't believe me.'

The news rang through the mountains, *'Liria! Liria!!'*

The heads of the tribe gathered together a-squat in a circle before the little white church.

Hil, a mere skeleton, but still a *zoti i shpis* (a house-lord), sat as by right in the tribe's parliament. And the Padre in brown Franciscan habit stood on the balcony of his tiny hospice. As the only man who could read and write, it was his duty to be present to record the tribe's decrees.

'It is a lie,' cried the old bairaktar. 'Never will I believe the Turks are gone. There has been no war. Eighty years old am I— and more—and I know that never have the Turks yet done a thing unless they were forced. I remember when the Muskovites came to the gates of Stamboul—I remember whenced the Nemtsi (Austrians) came into Bosnia. The Turks never give. Things are taken from them by arms. I, for one, will not go to

Scutari. This tale of "*Liria*" is a plot to assassinate the Christians!'

'By God, the *bairaktar* is right!' echoed the crowd.

Lulash rose on his knees and hurled a stone into the centre of the circle. 'On this stone and the cross I swear,' he said vehemently, 'that this is true. With my own eyes I saw the men of Vraka dancing and singing before the *Konak*. It is eighteen months since any one of them has dared to come into the town for fear of the Turks. It is the Seven Kings that have done this. There will be no more rule of the Padishah. It is *Korstituzioon*! 'He brought out the word triumphantly.

'Did you see him?' asked the *bairaktar*, eyeing him keenly.

'See whom?'

'Korstituzi?'

'No,' said Lulash, 'but...'

'Is the Vali Pasha there still?'

'Yes. But he will go. *Besa bes,* he will go,' cried Lulash, 'and the prisoners will be set free and the prison pulled down. It is *Liria,* I tell you, *Liria!*' His voice rang high over the hubbub of discussion.

In all the ragged crowd of half-wild men there was not one in whose family was not a tradition, centuries of sufferings at the hands of the Moslems—of death, of oppression, of vengeance.

The holy word '*Liria*' (Freedom) stirred even the aged blood of the *bairaktar*.

'*Kioft levdue Krist!*' (May Christ have praise!), he shrilled in his cracked old voice. '*Rrnojt Shkypnia!*' (Long Live Albania!) And, raising his revolver high over his head, he fired all its six cartridges up in the air.

The Franciscan, from his balcony, fired his rifle over the

heads of the crowd. And in a moment, the air was a-whistle with bullets and the echoes thud-thudded back and forth across the valley.

'*Rrnojt Shkypnia!* '*Rrnoft Shkypnia!!*'

'Oy Padre!' cried the *bairaktar*, 'plenty of work for you now. The Seven Kings won't allow any stinking Mohammedans in the land now! You'll have enough baptizing to do—*besa bes!*'

'*Will* they all be baptized?' asked, doubtfully Deda—the youngest house-lord present.

'Of course they will if the *bairaktar* says so! Hold your tongue. He saw the sun before you were born!'

And amid laughter, shouting and firing, the day was fixed when the head-men of the tribe should troop down with their banner to Scutari, and swear fealty to the new order of things.

Drana and Gjoko sat under the little crooked oak and awaited Hil's return. Filthy and ragged they still were, and by force of habit, Drana spun incessantly. But she did not go up to the forest to cut wood. The old order of things had changed. The future was mysteriously golden and the present was bliss. Lulash's wife had given her a large lump of sheep cheese. She and Gjoko feasted together. A heavy thunderstorm had cleared the air and they were both conscious of unusual physical well-being.

Nor had they long to wait. Heralded by an echoing rattle of rifle-fire, the vanguard of returning tribesmen charged up the last slope—sweating, shouting, singing, and headed by the old *bairaktar* triumphant, upon a mule.

'Where's Bab?' asked Gjoko anxiously, as the tribesmen filed by and each turned towards the rocky track that led to his own lonely dwelling.

'Coming, coming!' cried a man, and burst out laughing. And slowly, last of all the throng, came Hil, leading a donkey.

Drana stood dumb with amazement. Hil came straight into the hovel, bringing the donkey with him.

'What a beautiful donkey!' cried Gjoko. 'Whose is it, Bab?'

'Mine,' said Hil.

'Did you steal it from the Turks, Bab, instead of the old one?'

'It was given me,' said Hil solemnly.

'Given! given!!' almost screamed Drana. 'Who gives donkeys? God! it is a miracle!'

She touched the donkey tentatively, as though to learn if it were real. And the donkey wagged its ears.

'It was a *yabandjee* (stranger) woman gave it to me——,' began Hil.

'The Blessed Virgin herself!' said Drana, and crossed herself.

'Who knows?' said Hil, 'there was a great crowd. Consul and officers and all the people of the town. We all went to the Konak. There were more than two thousand tribesmen there, all firing at once—*martinkas* and *altipatlers* (revolvers). I never saw anything so beautiful. But it was very hot, and as we were coming away, I fell by the roadside. And a *yabandjee* woman, with a dragoman, gave me water. And she asked about me. And I told her everything—how my brother was shot, and the donkey stolen, and the pig died, and the charcoal and the fever and the drought. Then I went to the Cathedral grounds with the others and we had as much as we could eat—bread and water-melons and rakia! And tobacco!! *Besa bes,* it is the first time I have had my belly full since the donkey was stolen.

And in the evening when we were making ready to start, came the dragoman with this donkey, and the pack-saddle, and the halter, and said the *yabandjee* woman sent it me—*and* two silver medjids!'—Drana gasped—'and I bought a candle and lit it in the Cathedral, for this is the work of some blessed Saint.'

'But we are excommunicated!' said Drana.

'How should the Blessed Virgin in Scutari know that the Padre up here has excommunicated us? And I bought some maize, and some salt and some coffee and some sugar!'

One after another Hil extracted the parcels from a sack on the donkey; 'and we must take good care of the donkey, the dragoman said, or the *yabandjee* woman will be angry.'

'God forbid!' cried Drana, at last finding voice; 'and are the Turks gone?'

'It is *Korstituzi*,' said Hil solemnly. 'All the prisoners are set free. And we have got a donkey.'

III

With the autumn came rain. The wells were filled, the springs flowed. Juicy green herbage sprang up between the rocks.

Folk in Scutari began to buy wood and charcoal for the winter. Hil, Drana, and the donkey worked hard. Sometimes they earned as much as ten shillings in a month. They were never, now, without enough maize and salt to live on. Sometimes they had a little coffee too.

Hil threw off the fever. Gjoko picked up strength.

All through the winter evenings folk hobnobbed together round the hearth. And most of all, they talked of Korstituzi. It would make a railroad, some said, and schools, and roads. There would be work for everyone—and heaps of food and money. No more toiling over the rocks to earn a few pence.

But the winter passed and the Turks had not yet gone nor shown any signs of going. No foreign king had come, and things went on the same as before.

'I told you it was a trick,' said the old *bairaktar*; 'the Postripa Moslems are as bad as ever. They swear Lulash has stolen a goat. He has not. We all know he has sworn his innocence on the altar along with five witnesses. But he cannot go to Scutari now or they will arrest him. And he is innocent. This is *Korstituzi*! We were fools to go to Scutari and feast and fire our rifles. It was a wedding without a bride!'

But Hil and Drana recked little of Korstituzi. They cherished the donkey. Hil padded the pack-saddle with sheep-wool lest it should rub sores, and the *yabandjee* woman or the Blessed Virgin be wroth. He made a great stack of dry beech-leaves for winter fodder, and when the snow came the donkey shared the hovel and roasted his sides pleasantly by the hearth.

With a donkey everything seemed possible. Hil borrowed money for maize to sow his little field and was slowly pay off the debt.

Some day he might even save up enough money to buy an old Martini and feel a man again. Nor did anyone, indeed, take interest in outside politics that did not affect the tribe.

Then one day came news that rang through the mountains. The Turks were demanding tax.

The *bairaktar* called a *medjliss* (parliament) on urgent business. Never, in all time, had the tribe been asked for taxes. The towns and the richer villages of the plains had paid for years. No roads nor public works had ever resulted, but Vali after Vali retired with his pockets well lined. But, hitherto, the mountains, where most folk wrung but a bare living from the rocks, had been free.

Now, one franc a year was asked for each sheep and goat, and a tenth part of each scanty corn crop was to go to the Government.

No one in Hil's mountains could grow maize enough to live. Few who had sheep and goats could afford to drink their milk. It was all made into white curd-cheese and sold in Scutari to buy maize and salt. Most of the tribe lived almost entirely on this and the salt whey they squeezed from the cheese.

Rakia they distilled from such vines as they grew, or from wild plums. For life on such low diet is hardly possible without stimulants, and for this reason they bought coffee whenever they had a few spare pence.

'This is *Korstituzi*!' said the *bairaktar*. 'What have these devils ever done for us? Never a road have they made in all the mountains! Never a school in the land have they made for our children! Now they want our money to buy gold braid for their officers and guns to kill us with. How can we pay them? I am *bairaktar,* and I have not tasted meat since St. Nikola. Coffee I have only for guests. They leave us to starve like dogs, and then ask for our money! Till they do something for us, we will do nothing for them!' He took the rosary from his belt and held up the cross that hung from it. 'By this cross, I swear that I will never pay money for Pashas to grow fat upon!'

A yell of applause followed. Head after head swore, and all the tribe was united.

Time passed and nothing happened. There were other

and richer districts from which money could be raised, and the Government did not think it worth while to send a battalion of soldiers to the mountains in order to collect a few pounds.

Hil and Drana did not trouble themselves. They had no sheep or goats and there was no tax on donkeys. As for their tiny maize crop, they had harvested it and stored it for the winter, and were simple enough to imagine that the tax could only be paid in kind and that the maize was quite safe.

In another week Hil would have paid off the debt on his maize and would begin to save up for a Martini. Drana helped him load the donkey and he went off cheerfully.

As he entered the town, a police officer cried to him: 'Oy, you! Stop there. What's your name?'

'Hil Marku.'

The officer noted it.

'What tribe?'

Hil hesitated.

'He's from Shlaku,' said a big zaptieh, 'I know him.'

'Shlaku,' said the officer, 'h'm—one of the men we want for taxes.' He spoke to the zaptieh next to him. Then he shouted to another approaching peasant.

Hil drove on his donkey to the charcoal bazaar with a gasp of relief. He had escaped. But he had been badly frightened. He sold his charcoal in a great hurry, hardly waiting to bargain. Then he paid the last *piastres* of his debt, bought twopenn'orth of salt, and started at once to return to the mountains.

'Hil, *moré*!' cried a woman who knew him, 'don't go by the *karakol* (police station)—they are arresting men for this cursed tax. Five Zadrima men have I seen taken.'

A cold terror seized Hil. More than ever he felt the loss of his Martini. He was unarmed, helpless. He turned down a side alley and hurried for the stony waste of the dry river-bed. Once across that he would find cover and get away safely.

He walked quickly, and the donkey, burdened by no pack, trotted gaily beside him.

They were already clattering on the stones when a voice of command rang out—'Halt!'

A zaptieh—the one who had recognised Hil at the entrance of the town—descended from the bank and stood in his path.

Hil gazed wildly round. Flight was impossible. It would have been followed at once by a bullet.

'Where are you off to, so fast?' asked the zaptieh.

'Home,' said Hil.

'You've got to pay your tax first. It's twenty-three piastres (3s. 4d.). You've sold your stuff'—he pointed to the donkey's empty pack-saddle—'and now you can pay up.'

'Twenty-three piastres!' gasped Hil—'twenty-three piastres!' 'Twenty-three piastres,' shouted the zaptieh, 'don't you understand Albanian? Twenty-three! Twenty-three!!'

'I tell you I haven't twenty-three piastres in the world,' said poor Hil. He fished under his shirt and pulled out the dirty little bag that hung round his neck together with an amulet against the evil eye.

'Look!' he said, and counted out the few battered *metaliks* (halfpennies) it contained.

The zaptieh laughed. 'Where's the money you sold your stuff for?'

'I owed it already,' said poor Hil. 'I tell you we can't grow enough maize for ourselves. How can I give any to the Pasha?'

'We've heard that tale too often,' said the zaptieh, 'none of you tribesmen have enough to eat, if one's to believe you. At any rate you can afford a fine donkey, and that's worth more than the tax any day. If you are quite sure you *won't* pay, I'll take the donkey.'

As he spoke he took hold of the halter of the donkey, which was standing quietly by, and pulled it.

Hil's world crashed to pieces around him. Nothing as terrible as the loss of his donkey had ever presented itself to his mind. It was his life, and Drana's, and Gjoko's, their present, their future, their only hope.

Blank terror seized him and turned him into a cringing suppliant. He prayed, he implored for mercy, pouring out a mixed torrent of entreaty to the zaptieh, and all his Saints. He offered all he had with him—his old knife, the salt, his few halfpence—he would bring firewood next week—or charcoal—he would—

The zaptieh, a big fair Bosniak, laughed loudly at the unhappy little man. 'All right,' he said teasingly, 'bring a whole bazarful of charcoal next week and pay up. And then you shall have the donkey back. We shall keep it, in case you forget. And the sooner you pay the better for you. For the donkey will be put up at the *han* and you'll have to pay sixpence a day for its keep. Good-bye—pleasant journey!'

He pulled the donkey, and turned to go. But the donkey planted all its four feet firmly and wagged its ears questioningly at Hil.

The zaptieh twisted the halter two or three times round his hand and wrist and tugged.

'My donkey,' cried Hil in agony—'only give me my

donkey. I'll pay you next week—*Pashe Zotin*, I'll pay you.'

'Pay now,' said the zaptieh, and he laughed again.

The donkey was lost for ever. Sixpence a day was more than Hil had ever dreamed of possessing. The madness of despair swept over him. Every fibre in his body contracted with rage; his face went livid; the pupils of his eyes were mere pin-points.

'Pay,' he yowled—'pay! *Derr e bir derrit* (swine and son of a swine)! I'll pay you!'

With the scream of a wild beast, he lowered his head, flung himself forward and butted the zaptieh in the belly with all his force. The man, completely taken by surprise, doubled up, gasping, clutched instinctively at his revolver, but his right hand was tangled in the halter, on which the frightened donkey plunged madly. And before he could recover Hil had borne him down in his furious onrush, had torn the revolver from his belt and fired four bullets straight into his breast.

Hil turned and fled. The sound of the shots would bring up the patrol. If he could but get across the river-bed he would find cover and be safe.

The terrified donkey clattered after him, dragging the dying zaptieh whose life-blood spouted scarlet on the stones; but, hampered by the weight, could not keep up with Hil's wild flight, and brayed aloud.

Even at the risk of his own life, Hil could not abandon the donkey. He checked a moment, opened the clasp-knife that hung at his belt, and cut the halter. The donkey darted forward and made for the well-known track to the mountains.

A shout rang over the plains. Hil swerved and made for the nearest thicket. Three bullets squealed after him.

It was very late that night when the donkey, its pack-saddle all awry, arrived at the little hovel. But Drana and Gjoko waited for Hil in vain. He lay dead in the little thicket, for the patrol did not trouble to follow up the game and see if the bullets had hit or missed: nor was his body found for two weeks. And then it was buried where it lay. For he was excommunicate.

So Hil indubitably lost his soul. And Drana and Gjoko lost Hil.

As for *Korstituzi*, it was short of three-and-four pence and a zaptieh.

[from: *The Cornhill Magazine*, New Series, London, Vol. XXXIV, January to June 1913, p. 676-688.]

Travels in Trueland:
An Ecclesiatical Episode

"**Terribul** massacres! 'Orribul atrocities!!" howled the newsboy, and from the Extryspheshul I learnt that in an obscure corner of Europe, the Plondites had made a cruel and dastardly attack upon their subject members of the Bobianite Church. A leading article assured us fervently that "these people were Christian just as we are." The British public had never before heard of the sect, but, reassured by the above statement, its great heart beat violently. The Bishop of London, from the pulpit, implored the Bobians to take a bright view of death. The Lord Mayor raised a Fund. And it was as a relief agent that I, who a year or two before had made a tour in the neighbourhood, found myself entering the town which was the centre of the disturbed district.

Outwardly all was quiet. Only the presence of a large number of the Plondite gendarmerie in their pink and canary uniforms showed things were not quite normal. The Gouvernador of the town received me politely. Our Foreign Office had arranged that complete liberty of action should be given to the relief agents, with the sole proviso that they should not undertake any political or revolutionary propaganda. My passport was duly visé, and I was directed to the Palace of the Cephepisk or Head of the Bobianite Church, a bizarre building in the outskirts of the town.

After some delay I gained admission by a postern and was directed to wait in an ante-room while my credentials were examined. Meanwhile, I looked with interest at the barbaric scheme of decoration. Weirdly waving lines of blue and green covered the walls. The floor was covered by a rich blue carpet patterned with green blobs and waving arms. Doors and ceiling even were similarly adorned.

The Cephepisk himself entered shortly and greeted me with great cordiality. He was a reverend personage clad in a long black robe embroidered with a design similar to that on the carpet and the walls. And his silver locks flowed on his shoulders.

I rose as he entered. He waved me courteously to a seat saying, through his secretary, who had learned to speak English perfectly at an American Mission school: "I greet you as a brother. It is true that there are certain doctrinal differences between your Church and mine—but we both hate the Pope!"

Having thus determined a common Christian meeting ground, he was ready, he said, to give me all information, but first he must thank the great British nation which had come forward so nobly to the aid of what all the world must soon recognise as the only true Church.

I expressed a hope that the world was becoming more tolerant upon religious questions, and observing that he received this with marked coldness, hastened to condole with him upon the massacre and to hope that the number of victims had been exaggerated.

"Unfortunately," he sighed, "the massacre has not succeeded so well as we had hoped. We had reckoned that at least three-quarters of the population must perish. In that case the intervention of the Powers would have been inevitable; this land would undoubtedly have been freed and the ancient Tsardom of Bobia restored. As it is, more than half have survived and will remain under the Plondite yoke till further and more successful efforts are made." He sighed again and gazed at the ceiling.

"But—but," I gasped, considerably taken aback, "surely it was not—I mean I understood that there had been a deliberate and quite unprovoked attack on the part of the ruling race. Would his Grace kindly explain how the massacre came about?" "It was brought about," said the Cephepisk solemnly, "by the Cuttlefish Crisis. No more flagrant insult to religious liberty could be imagined. And that it was planned by Plonda is indubitable."

"The Cuttlefish Crisis—?" I murmured mystified.

"Are you then uninformed as to the tenets of any Church but your own?" asked the Cephepisk with lofty scorn.

"Oh, no," I replied hastily, "on the contrary I've studied the question of early heres—schis—I mean, of course, Churches, with great interest. But somehow the precise tenets of the Bobians have escaped my memory."

"Strange," said he, "for the Bobianite is the one authentic Christian Church and was founded in the first century by Bobe or Bobian, a poor fisher lad, a disciple of St. Peter, and by him baptised. Embarking as a sailor on a trading vessel he succeeded in the space of a fortnight in converting four of the crew so truly, that, when the ship was wrecked shortly afterwards, Bobian and his four converts alone were washed ashore, clinging to the mast and singing hymns which he specially composed for the occasion. The pagan natives, touched by Bobian's charm of manner, submitted joyfully to the rite of baptism in large numbers. But, unfortunately, owing to their deficient grasp of the language, they seem to have failed to comprehend the full meaning of Bobian's sermons. As Christmas Day approached, he saw, to his horror, that it was a feast day also of the natives. They began erecting altars and preparing offerings for a graven image of a highly obscene character.

"Bobian not merely refused to take any part in these ceremonies, he boldly excommunicated all those who did so, with the result that the whole population turned against him and his followers and drove them into the wilderness to starve.

"For a week they wandered without food or water, borne up solely by the knowledge of their own complete righteousness, and upon Christmas Eve Bobian fell exhausted among his followers. It was then that the miracle occurred. When he was at his last gasp, an Angel appeared to him saying merely 'Seek thy Salvation upon the Sea Shore.' And Bobian arose and went there. And as Christmas Day dawned, a wave broke at his feet, casting up a cuttlefish of enormous size. The starving men stewed it in the large shells which abounded upon the beach and thus initiated the Christmas feast of the Bobians.

"Nor did the miracle cease there. The Pagans, coming a fortnight later, were struck dumb when they beheld each wave that broke casting up a cuttlefish at the feet of each true believer. Bursting into tears, they threw themselves as penitents at Bobian's feet and he received them again into the bosom of the Church. Whereupon the sea became greatly agitated and cast up thousands of cuttles till there was one for each sinner saved. Thus was instituted the Feast of the Casting up of Cuttlefish and the Bobian Church established for ever. Green and blue, the colours of the sea became those of the Church, and the Mystic Cuttlefish," he pointed to the design on his robe and the walls, "is its symbol. Like the Church, when attacked it scorns to reason with the enemy. It pours floods of ink, concealing itself so that he can only retire vanquished and impotent."

The Cephepisk here made a holy sign and paused for breath.

"Miraculous indeed," said I, "but what was the crisis his Grace spoke of?"

"Ever since that day," continued the Cephepisk, "enemies have striven to shake the faith of the Bobianites. Nestorians, Sabellians, Arians, Monophysites, Moslems, Anabaptists, Papists, Buddhists. Presbyterians, Plymouth Brethren, Jews, Wesleyans, Bogomils, and Seventh Day Adventists have sent mission after mission. None have succeeded in penetrating the black and mystic cloud within which the faith of the Bobians protects itself. Many times has the nation, alas, been conquered. Many times have Bobians wandered forth and founded colonies of which this is one. But, never, never have they allowed a ray of external light to penetrate their beloved Church. For years our rulers, the Plondites, have striven to convince us that the Cult of the Cuttlefish is false, but in vain.

"Recently they have changed their tactics, and began what in their jargon they term 'Fishpolitik.' They declared that the cuttlefish of the coast were infected with enteric and forbade their being brought inland under severe penalties."

"But perhaps they were," I ventures,— "in our land the oysters—" "Sir!" cried the Cephepisk loudly, "Who ever heard of a cuttlefish dying of enteric? The claim is ridiculous. It is a deliberate and most foul attack upon our Church. The Gouvernador first addressed me on the subject, and at his request I gave my flock a dispensation, allowing them to substitute fresh-water mussels for the Christmas Feast, but at the same time reminded him that as my authority is purely spiritual, I could not be responsible for results. To my flock I was careful not to mention politics, merely pointing out to them that, unless well-boiled, mussels are apt to disagree. This, I regret to say, was an unfortunate remark, for with a view to saving their offspring from dyspepsia, a gallant band of the faithful managed to land and smuggle across the frontier a remarkably fine lot of cuttlefish carefully packed in top-boots. Alas! They were detected by the Octroi men, and these insolent minions of Plonda not merely destroyed the fish, but confiscated the boots which contained them. Unfortunately, I was not there to preach peace. Our men resisted. A fight ensued which resulted in the massacre which has shocked the civilised world. What will happen? One thing only is certain. The Church of the Bobians will never yield. The rest is in God's hands." He folded his hands upon his stomach and gazed upwards.

"To an anthropologist like myself," said I, profoundly moved, "the question of the cuttlefish is in the highest degree interesting. But from the strictly theological point of view, may I ask what it has to do with Christ and His teaching?"

"That," cried the Cephepisk angrily, "is a question which I must utterly decline to discuss with a layman."

"Nevertheless," I persisted, "would not a union with some

larger branch of the Christian Church be possible? And make for safety? Many of the Anglican Bishops, including him of London are expressing the warmest admiration for the Bobian Church."

"Necessarily," said the Cephepisk, "since it is the only True Church. And I shall be pleased at any time to receive them into its bosom." Feeling that the clouds of the Mystic Cuttlefish were obscuring the air, I dropped the subject.

"Could his Grace give me any idea of the future plans and aspirations of the Bobians?"

"Certainly," replied the secretary at once, "we demand the union of the Bobian nation and all the Bobian colonies and the reconstitution of the Great Bobian Empire of the fourth century."

"And," added the Cephepisk, "the extension of the True Faith throughout the world. Our programme is very simple."

"But," I urged, "here, for example, where the Bobians form such a small minority, not a quarter I am told of the whole pop——"

"A minority!" cried the Cephepisk and his secretary together, "A minority! The whole country is Bobian!"

"Nevertheless," I maintained, "the Plondites are the ruling power, and, judging by recent unfortunate events, are numerically stronger."

"Politically, and, according to text-books compiled by themselves, that is so. But in truth the bulk of the people here are not Plondites at all."

"But what are they then?"

"They are Plondophone Bobians!" cried the Cephepisk

triumphantly. "Conquered and overrun by the Plondites in the twelfth century the oppressed inhabitants, alas! forsook their own faith and language for that of the victor. My poor mother even spoke Plondite, and taught it to me as a child; but I have been careful to forget it. In her day the Church unfortunately had no schools, and the poor woman was never taught to speak the right language. Ethnographically this land is solid Bobian, as is proved by a survey made by experts from Petersburg and a map constructed by myself."

The secretary pulled a cord, and a large map of Europe was unrolled before me, almost entirely chequered with blue and green. A few spots even adorned the British Isles.

"I had no idea," said I, "that the Bobians were so widely spread."

"Few have," sighed the Cephepisk. "But what with Francophone Bobians, Teuto and Slav phone Bobians, a certain number of Anglophones—of which you, judging by the colour of your hair and eyes, are probably one—and a large amount of Crypto-Bobians concealed in fanatical lands, we amount to at least two hundred million souls."

Then why on earth do you allow yourselves to be massacred?" said I.

"All that we are at present able to do," said the secretary, "is to emphasise our position by inducing massacres, and to trust that the Great Powers will see justice done to us."

I remembered a former visit to a certain coast town, where a Plondite inhabitant complained bitterly of Bobian oppression.

"But what," I asked, "about the position of affairs on the Cerulean coast? There I was told it was just the other way round. The Plondites complained that they had to wear green and blue and send their children to a Bobian school——"

"Of course they had to!" cried his Grace testily. "Have I not just explained to you that racially the Plondites do not exist? That they are all Bobians?"

My brain reeled. I felt that the arms of the mystic cuttlefish were choking me.

"But all this is very awful," I said.

"It is," said the Cephepisk solemnly. "All I can do is to labour upon the spiritual side and teach the people that it is their first duty to die for the God-of-their-fathers."

"But why? Why? Why?" I cried desperately. "Why not teach them to live for the God of the Universe?"

"What!!!!" cried the Cephepisk in a voice so loud that the windows rattled.

"Why not teach them to live for the God of the Universe?" I repeated firmly.

The Cephepisk and his secretary conferred together. "His Grace," said the secretary presently, "is deeply shocked by your impiety. He bids me say that though he is amply aware that the doctrines of all the religious sects in England are erroneous, yet he thinks that in common decency you ought to be prepared to die for the God-of-your-fathers, no matter to which you may belong. He desires me to ask you if this is the case."

"Now look here," said I. "Tell his Grace that my family gave up the God-of-their-fathers ever so long ago. In my great-grandfather's time, In fact. The drawback of a God-of-your-fathers is this. His sphere is far too limited. He has next to nothing to do. He cannot take wide views of the world. He imagines that nothing but his own corner is of any importance, and the consequence is he spends pretty well all his spare time picking quarrels with the God-of-their-fathers next door. No. Don't interrupt! It is a fact. We had a God-of-our-father. No one ever saw him, but there was a little shrine, something like a dog-kennel on legs in the back garden, and my poor, dear great-grandmother spent a lot of her time decorating it and putting offerings in it. Well, if the God-of-our-fathers would only have kept quiet there and been satisfied to mind his own business, it would have been all right. But he was perpetually over the garden wall making mischief next door. The rows between him and the God-of-the-people-next-door were something awful. They quarrelled about everything—about the pettiest details— about candles—about what colour their servants' petticoats should be—about whether shrines should be whitewashed or gilt. The more you gave them, the more they wanted. They would hardly trouble to keep things even tidy at home, but they would go out on foraging expeditions and come back with captives, particularly women and young girls. At one time in fact there were massacres as bad as the one here, and the God-of-next-door's-fathers tied one of our family to a post and burnt him alive. When my great-grandfather saw the God-of-his-fathers was getting restless again, he made up his mind to stand it no longer. He waited till great-grandma had gone to the 'Movies' and he went into the garden and chivied the God and pulled down the shrine and made it into a rock-garden, which happened then to be all the rage. Poor great-grandma was very much distressed for a while, and even went on making offerings in a biscuit tin in the scullery. But the God-of-our-fathers never dared come back. My great-grandfather replaced him by the God of the Universe, and peace reigned at last. Not one quarrel have we had with next door since."

"And had you received no benefits at all from the God-of-your-fathers that you treated him thus impiously?" asked the Cephepisk sullenly.

"Benefits! Why, I told you, he and the Gods-of-other-peoples'-fathers perpetually shed blood and brought about misery. Not content with squabbling over the garden wall, they even at times would go far afield, leading large armies equipped apparently with harmless literature. But if the aborigines refused to read it or objected to the conduct of those who brought it, firearms were produced. Terrible fights ensued. Each side screamed for help to the God-of-his-fathers, who supplied him with poison gas, bombs, aeroplanes, submarines, torpedoes, dynamite, electriclite, toxophilite, perannolite, or some other new explosive every few weeks. Both sides, each burning with desire to save the unhappy aborigines from each other's evil influence, died in thousands for the God-of-their-fathers. As for the aborigines, some of them were wiped out altogether. It was a state of things which simply had to be put a stop to."

"And which side usually prevailed?" asked the Cephepisk in a level voice, gazing at me with a snake-like eye.

"The one that was best armed," said I.

"Quite so," said the Cephepisk. "That, I have strong reason to believe, will shortly be our case. Only thus can we hope to take our share in the White Man's burden, which, if I understand rightly, consists mainly of dead black men—and their inheritance. With the help of the God-of-her-fathers, Bobia will one day take her place in the sun. What if nine-tenths of the population should perish, provided that Bobia ultimately enjoy this inestimable privilege? So have I always preached to my people. So shall I continue to preach."

"But how can the nine-tenths who are massacred enjoy anything at all?" I persisted.

"They die knowing that their children will exploit the world! And father should be proud to give his son for such a purpose. And each father should bring up his son with this idea."

"That he ought to be massacred for the benefit of the next generation? But, my dear sir, then you never arrive. It is a case of 'biscuit to-morrow but never to-day,' as the Red Queen said to Alice."

At this moment the loud clangour of the monastery bell summoned the Cephepisk to his Cephepiskopal functions.

He consulted with his secretary for some moments in a hoarse whisper.

"His Grace," said the latter stiffly, "says he reckons that were it not for the fact that twenty caravans of flour and ten mule loads of shirts, combinations and handknit socks have just arrived, and that the Gouvernador absolutely refuses to allow them to be distributed by anyone but yourself, he could scarcely reconcile it with his conscience to permit you to come into contact with his innocent flock. He has certain knowledge that you are a member of a dangerous atheistical sect which he has not yet identified. Were it possible he would prefer, for once, to follow the example of a certain branch of the Church of England, which, he gathered from your papers, would not allow its buns and coffee to be distributed to the British Army save by communicants. Circumstances being, however, as they are, he suggests that I shall be present at your work to render you all the assistance which you evidently greatly need."

"With such an assistance," said I, bowing, "the work

cannot fail to proceed to his Grace's satisfaction. Pray thank his Grace for his extraordinary condescension, and say that I trust I may one day again have the honour of listening to his most illuminating discourse."

The Cephepisk, somewhat mollified, bowed with dignity as he sailed from the room. And I went with the secretary to search for suitable quarters for the relief work.

[from: *The International Review*, London, 1919, p. 33-40.]

Ritual Nudity in Europe

The very interesting article on *Nudity in Indian Custom and Ritual* in the Journal R.A.L, Vol. XLIX recalls to my mind two examples of ritual nudity related to me in North Albania in 1913. In neither case did I see the ceremony performed, but I was told of it as being by no means uncommon among the more remote mountain tribes. One of my informants was an Austrian priest who was making a careful study of the customs of the tribes among whom he had worked many years. He had himself seen the ceremonies. My dragoman, a native of Scutari, assured me that it was an accurate account.

I.   When a new house is built and is ready for habitation, the hearth has to be kindled for the first time ceremoniously. The fire is laid on the hearthstone: no person may remain in the house; the family gathers outside; the house-lord (*zoti i shpis*) strips stark naked, takes a loaded pistol and enters the house alone. He fires the pistol into the specially prepared fire, and, when it burns up, goes out, dresses, and the whole family takes possession of the house.

II. When a new pair of oxen are yoked together for the first time the *zoti i shpis*, similarly, has to plough the first furrow with them nude. These are very probably the only nude rituals practised in Europe (if indeed they are still practised, as the regions have been devastated by war), and seem, therefore, worth recording.

I may add that the men living along the Drin and in the habit of crossing it by swimming by the aid of inflated sheepskins, showed no self-consciousness whatever about being seen nude. At Apripa Gurit I was ferried over the river in a rude dug-out. One of the ferrymen, who was stark naked, sat down by me and chatted affably. He undertook to guide us on to the next village, sent a boy back over the river to fetch his very best clothes, and sat talking to us till they arrived, when he took three quarters of an hour to array himself. On another occasion I was walking with the Franciscan of the Dushmani tribe, when ahead of us appeared a man ploughing in a most exiguous shirt, for the weather was very hot. The Franciscan, much embarrassed, shouted to him to clothe himself, for "a maiden is coming!" The man replied, "Let her come," and went on ploughing.

[from: *Man, Journal of the Royal Anthropological Society,* London November 1920, p. 171-172.]

The Serbs As Seen in their National Songs

The *Narodne Pesme* of the Serb peoples are justly celebrated. Few other nations can show such a complete national history sung by generation to generation and passed from mouth to mouth. Songs which tell of the kings of old extend through Turkish rule and survive to the present day. For the peasant in the outlying districts will still seize his *guzle,* spit on the peg when tuning - to prevent it from slipping - and yowl roughly metrical lines about passing events, to the buzzing accompaniment of his one- stringed instrument. The songs as a whole form a mirror in which the whole life of the people is reflected. The history may be confused with myth; details may be contradictory; but it is the version which the people have accepted as true. It is the one that has moulded them. It is told with a rough realism that is strangely vivid. We see the life of the feudal noble; what was his code of honour; what he wore, ate, and drank. We live in the Middle Ages and see with mediaeval eyes. As in a "Movie Show" the ceaseless quarrels of the Balkan peoples pass before us and explain much of the problems of the Jugoslavia of to-day.

The Serbs, though they entered the peninsula first in about the fourth century A.D., for many centuries were dominated by Byzantine and Bulgar, for they were a tribal people and presented no united front to a foe. Not till the end of the eleventh century did they unite under the able leadership of the Nemanja dynasty and gain power which they extended and retained for over two centuries, and which culminated in the reign of Tsar Stefan Dushan (1336-1356), who spread his empire wide over the Balkans. Great Serbia might have lasted longer than the twenty years of Dushan's reign but for the fatal weakness of the system of semi-independent chieftaincies.

Vividly do the ballads relate how their rivalries rent that empire but a few years after Dushan's death. Tsar Dushan lay a-dying, runs the tale. Of all his Serb Voyvodas none were with him save Protopope Nedyelko and Kralyevitch Marko. And the glorious Tsar asked them: "To whom shall I leave my Empire? Should I leave it to my son Urosh, he is but a child and knoweth not how to rule. There are powerful folk in our land. They will slay my Urosh and fight each other for my Empire. Should I give it to Protopope Nedyelko, the priests will rise against him and will slay both him and my Urosh. To thee, then, oh Marko, my trusty henchman, will I leave it!" But Marko said: "My Lord! Leave me not thine Empire. Mine is an accursed line! When my dear father, Kralj Vukashin, and my uncles, Goyko and Uglesh, learn thy death they will fight one another for thine Empire. One will cry 'Tis mine!' and the second 'Tis mine,' and the third 'I yield to no man!' And they will slay thy Urosh." Then the Tsar bequeathed his Empire to the care of Marko till Urosh should be grown. And he died. And Goyko and Uglesh claimed the crown, and Marko's father, Kralj Vukashin, sent for him. "Would'st know what like he was? He was wrapped in a dark cloak; his fur cap was thrust down to his eyes, and he looked forth grimly and askance." When he heard that the crown was not for him he drew his sword that he might slay his dear son Marko. Marko, in truth, only saved himself by headlong flight to Prizren on his steed Sharatz. And there for seven years he guarded well the young Prince. When the seven years were past, Marko went to the plain of Kosovo, and with him to took Tsar Stefan's crown and his son, Childe Urosh. "When they came to the church of Grachanitza there was gathered a great multitude, and thither came, too, Kralj Vukashin, and his dear brethren, Goyko and Uglesh. And with Marko came Protopope Nedyelko to tell them whose should be the Empire. Nedyelko told how the Tsar had bidden them cast up his crown to heaven and see upon whom it should fall. Fiercely angered was Vukashin. He seized the crown in his white hand and hurled it to the clouds. And it fell upon Childe Urosh. Three times did Vukashin cast up the crown and thrice fell it upon Urosh. Then Vukashin drew his sword and would have slain both Urosh and Marko, but Marko seized the lad and leapt upon his fiery Sharatz and fled to Prizren." And when seven more years were past and Urosh was of age to reign, Marko left him and went to his castle of Prilip. And when Marko had gone, there came to Prizren Vukashin and his brethren and feigned friendship. They hailed young Urosh as the Golden Crown of Serbia and prayed that he would come a-hunting with them upon the Shar mountains. "And by the side of a lake Vukashin loosed a falcon and cried to Urosh to see how the bird would swoop upon a fish. As Urosh looked, Vukashin swung up his war-club and smote Childe Urosh between his black eyes and cast his body into the lake." And with him ended the Nemanja line and the Great Serbian

Empire. Many provinces at once broke loose. The songs tell of mighty Voyvodas, each powerful in his own district. And at this time not only were the Serbs divided amongst themselves, but the whole peninsula was rent in pieces by the rival claims of Bulgar, Greek, and Albanian. Each hated each more than they hated any outsider. Then, as to-day, each was prone rather to call in foreign aid than to unite against a common foe. The Turk first entered Europe as the ally of the Greek, against the growing power of Tsar Dushan, while, all unconscious of their fate, the Balkan princelings continued their internecine fights.

The next Serb ruler, over a greatly diminished Serbia, was the much be sung Tsar Lazar. His origin is dubious. The songs make him Dushan's serving man. Tradition says he was Dushan's illegitimate son. Tsar Dushan, runs one song, names Lazar as his successor at a feast which he gives to the mighty Voyvoda Yug Bogdan, and his nine warrior sons, and asks old Yug to give him his daughter in marriage. Here, though the details are not compatible with the song which tells of Urosh's nomination to the throne, the spirit of the age is doubtless truly pictured. In most of these tales, what have struck the singer most forcibly are the jealousies and quarrels of the chieftains. Here is a vivid snapshot: "What gift shall I make to the Tsar's serving man, Lazar Nemanitch?" asks old Yug Bogdan, when Lazar serves him with wine mingled with honey in a golden goblet. "'An thou wilt reward him,' says the Tsar, 'give him thy daughter, the maiden Militza, to wife and I will give him my crown!' When old Yug heard this, he looked at his nine fiery sons the Yugovitches. And they, stiff-necked and angry, looked at each other. And they leapt from the ground, snatched the swords from their scabbards, and rushed upon Lazar. Lazar fled to another room and made fast the door and the nine Yugovitches hurled themselves against it in vain. And back they rushed to the dining-hall and turned their swords upon the Tsar." The Tsar, however, succeeds in calming them by appealing to certain old books of prophecy. Old prophecies are frequently used in the ballads to account for events. When the Yugovitches find the thing is fated, they accept it, as Balkan people are apt to do to this day. Lazar, in due course, weds Militza and becomes Tsar.

His throne is no easy seat. The quarrels of the Voyvodas continue. Each, in fact, was all-powerful in his own domain. From the Canon of Stefan Dushan (1340) we learn that the peasants were tied to the noble's land; had to give him two days' work a week and extra work in hay time and vintage and paid tax. The noble might even build his own church and keep monks under his control. Save the dime, the noble paid no tax, but gave military service. And his serfs were his conscripts. Lazar was soon in difficulties with his turbulent and powerful Voyvodas. "The Serbs," as the songs frequently remark, "are hard drinkers, and when they have drunk they fight fiercely." We see Tsar Lazar "at his wine in the fair castle of Krushevo. And when the glorious Tsar had drunk a plenty of wine, he 'gan sing, and all his nobles watched him and none durst sing against him, save Voyvoda Milosh. And Vuk Brankovitch (Tsar Lazar's son-in-law) shouted: 'Dost see, oh lord Tsar, thine henchman! Of all thy court, none dare sing against thee save Milosh! If thou wilt hearken to me, to-morrow wilt thou hang him before the white church!' And glorious Tzar Lazar swore in his drunkenness: 'Seize him, dear lads! Bind me mine enemy!'" And they seized and bound Voyvoda Milosh and would hang him on the morrow. Militza, the Tsaritza, however, begs his life, or at least that he may not be hanged at Krushevo. And eventually the Tsar pardons him.

Lazar suffers, too, from his ferocious brothers-in-law, the nine Yugovitches. Again we find him giving a feast and placing his guests, with great care, in order of precedence, a very necessary precaution or a fight was sure to follow. We note, too, that, as a safeguard against poison, the Tsar's serving man tasted each wine cup before him. Then Tsar Lazar cried to his nobles, "See here, my Voyvodas! We sit and drink cold wine in plenty and live as lords, but nowhere do we build holy churches or monasteries." The Voyvodas, as usual, disagreed upon the question. The virtuous Milosh, however, pleases the Tsar by proposing to build a church at Ravanitza. "And they drank cold wine and the Tsar ordered his Voyvodas, and the Voyvodas ordered their Knets and Knezhes. And these summoned a thousand builders and a thousand young labourers and set over them Radé, the master-builder. And the nine Yugovitches were appointed to feed the workmen and pay them a ducat a day and three *okas* of wine that they might celebrate the mass on Fridays and Sundays. But alas! "Profiteering" is no new invention. "The wicked young Yugovitches sold all the Tsar's beer and took the Tsar's money. They paid the workmen but one *asper* a day, and gave but one little glass of wine. So that they could observe neither Friday nor Sunday, nor the day of St. Elijah who hurls the thunder, nor of St. Mary who sends the lightning." This curious description of the Virgin is not infrequent in the songs. It must be remembered that the Serbs were not converted to Christianity till the ninth century, and then in the wholesale-baptism fashion, which is more of outward ceremony than inward enlightenment. To return to the building of Ravanitza:

the master-builder, furious, complains to Tsar Lazar. Lazar, equally furious at the trick played upon him, at once orders all nine of his brothers-in-law to be hanged. "'As for old Yug,' he cries, 'tear out his black eyes; pull out his teeth; cut him in four pieces and hang them on a tree!'" But Militza the Empress again plays peace-maker, and begs the lives of her father and brothers. Tsar Lazar pardons them, and apparently they escape scot-free. He is neither the first nor the last to suffer from "in-laws," and there is much human nature in the tale, which shows, also, the impotence of a ruler when a number of his so-called subjects are independent despots in their own provinces.

The united and disciplined army of the Turks thus met a nation divided among itself. Tsar Lazar at first made terms with the Turks and furnished the Sultan with a Serbian contingent which fought for him in Asia Minor. Several of these were executed by the Sultan, for looting when it was forbidden, and the rest of them on returning to Serbia urged Tsar Lazar not to submit to a rule so unreasonable. Tsar Lazar then gathered a great army and met the Sultan's forces on the plain of Kosovo (1389). But so little control had he over his men that, as the song tells us, not one of the nine Yugovitches would obey the Tsar's order that one should abide in the white castle and guard the Empress. A quaint ballad tells of the fall of the Serbs and strives to explain it away by making out that it was fated. St. Elijah, in the form of a grey falcon, drops a letter from the Virgin Mary into Tsar Lazar's lap. The letter asks him: "Dost wish for the Kingdom of Heaven or would'st thou an Empire on earth? Would'st thou an Empire on earth, saddle thy steed and girth him tightly. Gird on thy sword. Charge down upon the Turks. So shall the Turkish army fall before thee? Would'st thou the Kingdom of Heaven, make thee a church at Kosovo and give there the Holy Communion to thine army. Then will thine army fall and thou with it, oh Tsar!" The Tsar ponders these very unfair conditions and considers which is the better bargain. "An earthly Kingdom," he reflects, "is but for a little while. The Kingdom of Heaven is for ever!" For his soul's sake he chooses the destruction of Serbia; and twelve Bishops give the Communion to the army. Each Voyvoda is described in the song as leading his own army. It is highly probable that there was no concerted action. The Balkan people are usually their own worst enemies, and Kosovo was no exception to the rule. Vuk Brankovitch, the Tsar's son-in-law, who had quarrelled ceaselessly with the other Voyvodas, deserted to the Turks with his twelve thousand men, and the Serbs lost the day. "Why askest thou me of Vuk the accursed?" says the song. "Cursed be he and he that begot him. Cursed be his stock and his seed. He betrayed his Tsar at Kosovo and took with him his twelve thousand fiery warriors!" Balkan history up till to-day is filled with Balkan chiefs and rulers who, in order to gain power over their neighbours, have thrown in their lot with an outsider. Vuk, says one song, "went to the Sultan at Stamboul, and the Sultan loves him as his own son." He takes Tsar Lazar's son Urosh to Stamboul as prisoner and casts him into a prison, where "he lamented night and day. In lordly fashion was he used to live, and here there were serpents and scorpions." Under promise of a heavy ransom Vuk takes young Urosh back to his mother, Tsaritza Militza, at Krushevo. He calls himself Bankovitch Bey and treats her with great brutality. (But perhaps this is because she was his mother-in-law?) Young Stefan Lazarevitch, however, Tsar Lazar's elder son, comes to the rescue and slays

Vuk. Vuk was buried at Krushevo, and, according to tradition, the Turks burned lamps on his grave till, in the nineteenth century, Krushevo again became Serbian.

In the next song series we find Stefan Lazarevitch reigning as suzerain to Sultan Bajazet, drinking wine with the Sultan and giving him his sister in marriage. And the Sultan permitting her to remain a Christian. Nor was he singular in his friendship for the Sultan. Marko Kralyevitch, the best beloved and most be sung of all Serb heroes, was a staunch friend of the Turks. Never, perhaps, has a stranger national hero been selected. We have seen that Marko was on the worst terms with his father. When Vukashin usurped royal power, Marko retired to Prilip. A certain obscurity hangs over him at this time, but it would seem that he early became an ally of the Turks. It has been suggested that he expected to be chosen Tsar on Vukashin's death, and so bore Tsar Lazar no love and gave him no help. It is even possible that he was on the Turkish side at Kosovo. My Montenegrin guide, a great ballad singer, always explained that when Marko was on the way to Kosovo, his steed Sharatz stumbled and went lame, and so they arrived too late. Otherwise the Serbs would certainly have won. The bulk of the songs, in fact, relate to Marko's exploits as faithful servant of the Sultan.

The Marko of these ballads is of singular interest. In spite of his loyalty to the Turks the ballad makers have bestowed upon him all the qualities they most admired, and fashioned a sort of Serbian superman as a pattern of perfection to all who came after. The human Marko stands out clear from his supernatural adjuncts, and we have a striking picture of a mediaeval warrior. Bloodthirsty, cruel, and revengeful to an extraordinary degree; cunning and apt to win by treachery; drunken and violent, he has yet been held up as a model to youth for centuries, and his example held to warrant many crimes. Often have I been told "Drunkenness wrong, lady? But Marko was drunk every day!" In the war of 1912-13 I actually heard the cutting off of prisoners' noses justified by the fact that Marko cut people up. In the very popular ballad of the Fair Roksanda, Marko and two of the Voyvodas go together to the house of Lek Kapetan and ask that the fair Roksanda shall choose one or other of them as husband; the other two to be bride-leaders at the wedding. Roksanda, an independent young woman, says frankly she will have neither. All three Voyvodas rush in a fury from the house. "And lo, the Devil put it into Roksanda's head to walk in the meadow, with her twelve maidens. And Marko said: 'Turn thy face, oh maiden Roksanda! My sister at Prilip will ask what like art thou.' Then did fair Roksanda betray herself. She turned towards Marko and he seized her right arm and cut it off at the shoulder, and gave it to her left hand to hold. And he dug out her eyes and thrust them in her bosom and cried: 'Choose now, Roksanda, whom wilt thou have.'" My guide, who called this a love-song, always maintained that Marko was quite right.

Marko in the songs is the Sultan's right-hand man, is given *bakshish,* and allowed to drink wine in Ramazan. His sworn brother is a Moslem, and, true to type, he even persuades the Sultan to lend him a troop of janissaries in order to fight against a Christian Prince, Mina of Kastoria; in history, Musacchi, an Albanian chief. We thus see how under Turkish rule the Balkan people continued to fight each other and even called in Turkish aid. On one occasion Marko employs a smith to forge him a fine sword, and to make sure he shall never make so fine a one for another, he cuts off the unhappy smith's hand. Marko has, however, some compensating good qualities. He is lavish with his money, though we had better not ask how he obtained it. He is merciful to the poor; hastens to help his friends in distress, and is always loyal to his lord the Sultan. And he died in the Sultan's service.

Nor was he the only one who served the Sultan. In spite of the curse, Vuk Brankovitch's descendants flourished for a time as rulers of Serbia under the Turk. George Ban Despot, in fact, thought Roman Catholicism far worse than Islam. When the Hungarian champion John Hunyades (called in the songs Sibinya Yanko) came to fight the Turks, the song says "George Ban Despot asked of Yanko, 'If by God's will thou should'st conquer the Sultan, what manner of faith wilt thou leave us?'" And Yanko said that they should serve the Mass and believe in the Pope of Rome. Then George Ban Despot asked the Sultan and the Sultan replied: "I will build churches and mosques, one beside the other. He that will bow himself, let him go to the mosque. He that will cross himself, to the church." And when George Ban Despot heard this, he betrayed Yanko. George did, in fact, on more than one occasion fight on the Turkish side against Hungary. The Sultan kept his promise about the churches. The monastery of Devich dates from this period, and the frescoes in many an old pre-Turkish church have not suffered so badly at Turkish hands as did the decorations in our own cathedrals in the days of Cromwell.

The next ballad group deals with the Hayduks or brigand heroes of the fifteenth and sixteenth centuries, and comes down to quite modern times when Grand Voyvoda Mirko, father of King Nikola of Montenegro, celebrated the border raids of the middle of the nineteenth century, and gloated over Turkish heads stuck on stakes, and carried as trophies round the villages. Brigandage was very popular. Except on the main trade routes, the Turks kept little or no order. The ballads, especially those of Bosnia, give us many a lively picture. The life was lucrative and sporting. The state of the tracks made it impossible in winter, and the season opened on St. George's Day when the band, which had lived on plunder during the winter, met again at its trusting place. It was a life which suited the lazy and adventurous nature of the people.

A much-sung hero, Old Man Novak, lived on the mountains above Sarajevo, and drove a thriving trade for years, retiring in his old age to the Bocche di Cattaro, where he died honoured and respected. Old Man Novak tells us that he turned brigand because of the tyranny of cursed Jelena, the wife of George Brankovitch, the Serb ruler. "Three whole years did not I toil for her, and not a franc nor a farthing did she pay. That, oh brother, I would have pardoned her, but when the building of Smederevo was finished, she began to gild the doors and windows, and put a tax on each house. I was a very poor man. Naught had I to pay the tax with. I picked up the hoe with which I worked, and off I went to the brigands." A curious little picture of feudal oppression. The peasant, as a serf under the Turks, probably suffered at first no more than he had done as serf under the Serb Voyvodas. For the Turks accepted things much as they found them and perpetuated old customs. In the sixteenth century, large numbers of Serb chiefs, especially in Bosnia, turned Moslem, and the "Turk" who, in the songs, oppressed the Christian is, in fact, usually a brother Serb. The Christian *rayah* who paid taxes and gave labour to the Moslem Pasha was in nine cases out of ten the Serb serf oppressed by the

Serb noble. We have seen how the young Yugovitches treated the workmen of Ravanitza. We find the "Christian" brigands had sworn brethren among the Moslems, and, though Old Man Novak had many a skirmish with Moslems, he is equally ready to fight Christians. On one occasion when very hard up, he goes down into Sarajevo with his handsome son, Young Gruitz, whom he sells to a wealthy Moslem widow as a slave. Gruitz, of course, bolts next day with all the plunder he can lay hands on. The tale is of interest as it shows that slave dealing was an accepted fact. When Novak wants a bride for Gruitz, he elects to snatch the bride of a Greek, Manoylo, ambushes him in a narrow pass, and kills him and many of the Greeks and Bulgars who form the wedding party. For Greeks, Bulgars, and Serbs hated each other as much under the Turk as previously, and it would never have occurred to Old Novak and his like to unite with Greeks and Bulgars against the common enemy. The idea, in fact, did not occur till 1912, and union then lasted but six months.

The ballads of Montenegro are almost all either war songs or tales of brigandage. Brigandage was, till 1870, the main livelihood of the country. My guide's great uncle was a pirate who plied between Cattaro and the Aegean. The Moslems on the Montenegrin borders of the Herzegovina were mainly Serbs who had turned Turk, and we find in the songs the Montenegrins alternately swearing brotherhood with them and plundering them. A continuation truly of the mediaeval rivalry of chieftains, exacerbated by religious differences. The hatred, in fact, of the Christian Serb for the Moslem Serb is one of the difficulties which has yet to be faced. The Moslems, too, have a collection of Serb ballads, and oddly enough, it is among them that we find the prettiest tales of domestic life. But as these do not concern the history of the land, we cannot now consider them.

In the historic ballads one thing stands out sharp and clear. It is that Balkan troubles have nearly all been due to Balkan inability to cohere. Over and over again is the mournful tale repeated? May the poets of the future have a less disastrous policy to sing about? There is territory enough in the peninsula for all its races - room for all to develop. Let us hope, above all things, that no desire to gain land at the expense of another Balkan race will in future tempt any one of these peoples to call in foreign aid against another. Up till to-day each, with hope of crushing a Balkan rival, has allowed itself to be made the cats-paw of one or other of the Great Powers, with the result that the ashes rather than the chestnut have been its portion.

[from: *The Contemporary Review*, London, No. 652, April 1920, p. 531-538.]

Because of the Berlin Congress:
A True Tale, Dedicated to the Drawers of Frontiers

The Berlin Congress dragged wearily along. Nominally, the Powers were met to settle the Near Eastern Question and to establish a possible peace. Nominally, in fact, this is the object of all Peace Conferences. Practically, however, each Power was there to outwit the other and make the best possible bargain for itself.

'Wheresoever the carcass is, there will the eagles be gathered together,' is a motto that might be inscribed at the entrance of many a Conference chamber.

The Turk, in 1878, was by no means a carcass. But he was sufficiently weakened for whole limbs to be torn from him with impunity. And the eagles—double and single headed—lions, cocks, and other beasts and wildfowl, scrambled with each other for the gobbets. Nor was this in any way surprising; for this Congress differed in no particular from any other that the world has seen.

The land was there to be divided for the benefit of the dividers. None took heed of the wishes of the human cattle upon it, save only when their wishes happened to coincide with those of a Power great enough to enforce its claim.

It was a brilliant game—as one in which such wits as Beaconsfield and Bismarck moved the pawns, was bound to be.

But even of such a game, the players tire at last. Bismarck announced that a special train was awaiting him, and could wait no longer. Some attribute this remark to Beaconsfield. In either case, the result was the same. The final decisions had to be made; the final frontiers drawn. What with claim and counterclaim; survey and re-survey; statistics convincingly proving one thing, and another set proving the converse; the draughtsmen had drawn and redrawn till they were sick of the sight of maps.

Finally, everyone being equally weary and no one foreseeing any further gains of importance to be acquired, it was agreed to split the remaining little differences, and split they were; for the resultant fragments were too small for any Power, worthy the title of Great, to take the least interest in. So the Powers retired, sated for the time being, to digest, boa-constrictor-like, their gains till their appetites should again awaken. And left the split fragments to adapt themselves to the situation as best they could.

★ ★ ★

Stoyana climbed the rocky track to her hut quickly, and breathing hard. Not the climb, but indignation made her pant.

"Free country indeed!" She cried scornfully, as she swung the empty water-barrel from her shoulders and let it thump on the threshold. "Free country! After all these years of fighting, and God knows what misery, they tell us we are freed from the

Turks, and give our village to Gospodar Nikita (Prince Nikola of Montenegro). Pretty freedom indeed!"

"What is the matter, woman?" asked Labud, her husband, coming from the door and drawing his long *chibouk* from his mouth. "What is all this noise about?"

"Noise!" cried Stoyana. *"You'd* make a noise, I should think! I went to the spring to draw water, just as I have done ever since I was married to you and came here, and there in front of the well were a lot of Schwab (Austrian) soldiers. Terrible men. They shouted at me and would not let me come near the water. And I shouted at them. Then there came an officer, a fine gentleman, with gold braid on him, and he spoke Serb, and told me I must not cross the frontier. I told him the spring belonged to our village, and we must have water. He says the spring doesn't belong to our village now, it belongs to his Emperor. I said, "Then where are we to fetch water?" He said, "That is not my affair." And he said, "Now, don't you forget what I've told you, and tell your man not to let me catch him across the border. Your village is Montenegrin now, and you are to stay in your own land." That is what he said. By God it is true! Ask Marinka and Danitza, if you don't believe me!" shouted Stoyana, pointing to two more indignant women, who also were returning from a fruitless quest.

Their voices rose in shrill complaint.

"Hold your tongues!" cried Labud roughly. Of all things in the world he hated to be pestered by the affairs of the *chelyad* (womenfolk). "If you can't get water there, you must go up to Gornyi Bunar for it." He withdrew into the house and shut the door.

"Gornyi Bunar! Gornyi Bunar!" said Stoyana indignantly.

"Just like a man! Twenty minutes farther to go,…and he calmly says, "Go to Gornyi Bunar." Men don't have to fetch and carry. A lot he cares."

But she durst not disobey; slung on her barrel again and started—this time climbing up the mountain—swearing between her teeth as she went.

Labud had said little, for he never discussed things with women; he merely gave orders. But he was truly filled with dismay by his wife's words. After years of guerilla fighting, he and his fellow clansmen had laid down their arms with the comfortable belief that now that the Turk was gone, earth would be a Paradise; that the Great Powers were almighty and beneficent beings, and would arrange all for the best.

Their faith had been rudely shaken when they found that though Labud's village had been assigned to Montenegro, his cousins' lands had fallen to the lot of Austria. The tribesmen at once sprang to arms again, and only after fighting that was fiercer than ever, was peace forced upon them.

The Austrian occupation was completed. Labud returned from the mountains to his village with a vague hope in his peasant brain that the Gospodar and Russia would see justice done to them. But now, when he realised that the frontier line actually ran between the village and the spring from which it had obtained its water for centuries, he was puzzled and gravely uneasy. Angered too, he vented his anger on the innocent Stoyana.

Trouble was ahead. The upper spring belonged to another village. The village would object to sharing it. A village council must be called. And the fact that foreign soldiers were so very near his home filled him with anxiety. Vaguely he wondered, as many another has since done, whether the results of a war in any way compensate for its miseries. Why could not the Seven Kings who, so he believed, ruled European affairs, have made inquiries before they made this unjust and intolerable frontier? Anyone could have told them if they had but asked. That he was a mere split difference, about which the Seven Kings neither knew nor cared, did not occur to him. Labud decided that he would call the village council at once, and send representatives to Cettinye to the Gospodar, who would certainly have the matter put right.

Several days passed. Troublous days, for the folk of Gornyi Bunar were by no means pleased to share their spring with another village. Just now it was all very well, but soon the heat and the drought would be on them and there would not be enough water for themselves, let alone for other people.

Labud smoked pipe after pipe, and none brought him counsel. The hut grew darker and darker. Night fell.

"Where are the boys?" he asked suddenly. "Where are Boshko and Liubomir? It is time the sheep were folded for the night."

"How should I know!" said Stoyana testily. She was busy with the supper in the big cauldron. "Now that I have to go all the way to Gornyi Bunar for water how can I ——"

"Hold your tongue, woman!" broke in Labud. As a Montenegrin of the old school, he never addressed his wife by her name. And Stoyana, as a modest woman, would rather have died than so far forget herself as to call him "Labud."

By way of stopping her complaints, Labud strode to the door and gazed out. The profound immensity of the blue night sky was all aglitter with stars, and along with them the world swung in space. The infinitesimally small question of the water supply of Gornyi Bunar made no difference whatever to the Universe.

Bleating and hustling over the rocky track, came the belated flock, following its shepherds.

"Oy Boshko! What do you mean by being so late? Do you expect me to wait supper all night for you? Get the sheep shut up, both of you, and look lively!" shouted Labud surlily.

"It's not our fault, father. By St. Peter, it is not! Liubomir and I have been miles after the sheep to-day. Three of them have gone astray——"

"And whose fault is that, I should like to know?"

"It was hot to-day, father. They are used to go and drink at the lower spring. They kept breaking away. We've been herding them back all day. Somehow, three slipped us. We've looked for them everywhere. I'm afraid they've gone over the frontier. We didn't dare go after them."

"And curse you for a couple of fools! Why the devil couldn't you see they didn't stray? I'll go and look for them myself!" cried Labud furiously. He went back into the cottage and took his long flint-lock gun from its hook. Then hesitated, for the carrying of arms across the border was strictly forbidden. "They can't refuse to give me my own sheep," he said uncertainly. He put the gun back, and started forth alone. And he never came back.

★ ★ ★

"Herr Hauptmann, may I speak to you?" said the corporal, saluting respectfully.

"What's the matter now?" asked the Captain of the frontier guard.

"Please, Herr Hauptmann, I reported to you this morning early, that the night patrol caught a man stealing sheep, and as he would not stop when they challenged him and tried to run away, they fired at him and, as it happened, killed him."

"Quite right, too!" said the Captain shortly. "They are celebrated *Hammeldiebe* (sheep stealers), these Montenegrins. We shall have to make an example of a few before they understand that they can't come raiding over the borders as they did in the days of the Turk."

"But if you please, sir, it seems now that they were the man's own sheep, after all. There is a woman here—come about an hour ago—she is carrying on something shocking—beating her breast and clawing her face. The sheep run down after the water, she says, and her husband he comes after them."

"Damnation! Then why in God's name couldn't the fellow have said so, when the patrol challenged him?"

"The patrol, please, sir, was all Hungarians, you know. They don't know the lingo of these parts. The man shouted at them a lot, they said, but they thought it was just his lip."

Alas! With the idea of preventing any fraternising by the army of occupation with the men across the new frontier, some brilliant genius had been struck with the idea of employing troops who could not speak the local tongue. And this was the first result.

Labud was dead, and nothing could undo it.

The Captain, genuinely touched by the sight of poor Stoyana's wild distress, and anxious, moreover, to avoid frontier trouble, did his best. Labud's poor body was treated with all honour. But the dark and sullen tribesmen, who came to bear it away shoulder-high upon a rough bier, received all his explanations and proffered compensation with a cold, dead silence. And it was with a foreboding of trouble that he watched the long procession trail back into the mountains, wailing as it went.

Then a silence settled upon the border. A silence so long and absolute that he hoped the affair was over and forgotten, until he was hastily summoned in the grey dawn after a moonless night, and saw the bodies of the corporal and one of his men swinging from the branch of a crooked oak, with purple faces and hideous protruded tongues.

Then he, in his turn, swore vengeance.

Neither the corporal nor his man had been concerned in the killing of Labud. And those who had killed Labud were only following orders. The machine devised at the Peace Congress—ignorant, inhuman, and relentless—had been set going, and had caught and crushed in its grinching cogs three innocent men who happened to be standing near. Three men had died, and undying hatred had been born. Had died, in truth, as many more will die—because of the United Wisdom and the Split Differences of a Great Peace Conference. It is at such that wars are made. For war is the result of an infinite number of small hatreds.

[from: *The Cornhill Magazine,* London, New Series XLIX, June to December 1920, p. 155-160.]

King Nikola of Montenegro

On March 1st, Nikola Petrovitch Njegushi, first and last King of Montenegro, died in exile at Antibes, in the eightieth year of his age. The last ruler in Europe to lead his own armies into battle, he was, in fact, the last of the mediaeval chieftains, and with him closes a whole epoch of history.

Modern Montenegro began with the rule of Prince Danilo I. in 1851. He was nominated to succeed his uncle Vladika Petar II., but said at once that he would not take holy orders and wished to marry. This raised an international question. There was nothing unusual in the recognition of a Bishop as head of a Christian unit in the Turkish Empire. But to permit a secular ruler was quite another thing. Russia so strongly supported Danilo's claim, however, that the Porte gave way. Danilo was made first Prince of Montenegro, and inheritance was decreed in the direct male line. The superstitious, so the peasants have often told me, foretold that the curse of God would follow Danilo's refusal of spiritual power in favour of marriage, and that no son would ever inherit. A prophecy which has proved strangely true.

Montenegro was still nominally part of Turkey, but Danilo

began energetically to reorganise it, and with the help of the Russian envoy, Medakovitch, drew up a code of laws which embodied ancient custom and was not superseded till 1888, and enforced them. The levying of a tax caused fierce revolt. "The Great Eagle(Vladika Petar II.) could not make us pay. Does this young cock think he can do so?" cried the tribesmen. But Danilo put down revolt with terrible severity. He was sure of supporters so long as he could pay them well, and scoured Russia, Austria and Paris in search of subsidies. But in enforcing his power he made many enemies, and he was murdered by a Montenegrin in 1860, leaving no son to succeed him.

The Code merits consideration, for it gives a vivid picture of the times in which King Nikola began his reign at the early age of nineteen, when summoned suddenly to replace his uncle, and enables us to realise how greatly he raised and civilised his people. "The person of the Prince as lord of the land is sacred. No Montenegrin for any reason must speak ill of his person or action. Any Montenegrin who insults the person or character of the Prince will be punished by death. Every traitor who treats with the enemy or causes revolt shall be shot, if his guilt be proved by two witnesses. Any Montenegrin has the right to shoot him." (This was probably the origin of the reign of terror which contemporary accounts describe, and which caused Danilo's death.) "In time of war every man must take up arms and march against the enemy. Any man too timid or indifferent to do so shall be deprived of his arms and of his rights and shall have to wear a woman's apron that all may know he has not the heart of a man." In order to stop the very frequent murders, article 37 enacted "Every Montenegrin who kills a man without motive or necessity shall be shot, and cannot be absolved by any payment of bloodgelt. It is permitted to any Montenegrin to shoot such a malefactor just as though he had killed the man's own brother."

"Should a man strike another without reason, with his foot or pipe (the long *chibouk)* the man struck has the right to kill his aggressor at once. Should he do so after two days have elapsed he will be treated as a murderer."

"The Montenegrins are accustomed to take blood-vengeance not only on the assassin but on his innocent relatives. Such vengeance on the innocent is now forbidden on pain of death. The assassin and no other must pay for his crime with his life." Blood vengeance was thus recognised but limited. The Code supported strongly the old tribal idea *of patria potestas.* "Should a son fail to respect his father and mother and give trouble, he shall be fined. Should he again disobey, he shall be imprisoned and flogged. A son may not leave his home during his father's lifetime without his father's consent." "Anyone refusing to pay the tax which has been imposed for the good of the country shall be put to death." The priesthood was fonder of leading raids than of doing its ecclesiastical duty, so the law said "Every priest must go to the church on Sunday, and keep it clean, and observe the Canons of the Church, and instruct the people as much as possible in our holy religion." But it was not till the "sixties that they were ordered to dress as priests and let their hair grow in Orthodox fashion.

A man whose wife was unfaithful was at liberty to kill her and her paramour, if he caught them together. Divorce, which had been extremely frequent, was prohibited. Theft was punished with flogging. Theft of Church property, with death.

In all there were 93 articles showing on the whole a

sincere attempt to soften the inherent savagery of the land, which in point of social development was in the early middle ages. Nothing in Nature stands still. It develops or atrophies. Cut off by force of circumstances from the rest of Europe, the Montenegrins had not only not advanced with it, but had probably retrograded as do animals which "turn feral".

Prince Danilo had transformed the land from a theocracy of a rude sort to a military autocracy, and as such young Nikola received it. Educated in Paris at the Lycée Louis le Grand there was then mentally a gap of several centuries between him and his completely ignorant people. A Russian Tsar is reported to have said there is no such thing as good despotism, but there may be a good despot. And a good despot Nikola honestly tried to be. The Code made his person sacred and gave him complete power of life and death. Nominally a check on the ruler was to be kept by a Soviet or Council of eighteen *voyvodas* (headmen). But each was obliged only to live three or four months in Cetinje so that the Soviet consisted usually of but four or five. They could propose laws but the final decision remained with the Prince. "Soviet Government" is spoken of nowadays as a new and wonderful invention. But, in fact, the Montenegrin council of elected headmen dominated by Prince Nikola was but a forerunner of the Russian Soviets dominated by Lenin, and is only a form of autocracy, bound to fall when the people become educated.

Young Nikola made sure that the Soviet should agree with him by making his father, the redoubtable warrior Mirko, its president, and his uncle Constantine, vice president. He strove to be father of his people, but it was as the father of the Code who had absolute power over his sons.

From the beginning he was inspired by an ideal. He aimed at reconstructing the ancient Serbian Empire and ruling as its Tsar at Prizren. Serbia was torn by internal feuds. Tsar Alexander of Russia called Nikola his "only friend". Russia and France both paid him a yearly subsidy. The early Vladikas had considered the Great Serbian Idea. Nikola devoted his life to it, and spared no pains or effort. But the star which he followed proved but a will o' the wisp and his life has ended tragically.

He married, so soon as he became Prince, Milena, daughter of Voyvoda Vukotich of Kchevo, to whom he had been betrothed in childhood. And the very young couple began their reign.

In a wholly illiterate land the minstrel has always been a power. He was the mediaeval forerunner of the cinema - a means by which propaganda may be spread with a minimum of mental exertion on the part of the audience. Nikola and his father, both poets, flooded the land with songs. Voyvoda Mirko detailed in crude verse the very gory details of the fights of the 'fifties and 'sixties, the slaughter and the head-cutting, and encouraged militarism. Prince Nikola sang of patriotism and instilled the Great Serbian Idea. His song, "Onward, onward, let me see Prizren - For it is mine, I shall come to my home!" has become a national song for all the Serb race. He made the wearing of the national cap compulsory for men and women, and the main teaching in such schools as existed was of the duty of avenging Kosovo. The handsome national costume was both Court and military wear. And he subtly instilled into his people the belief that they were the flower of the Serb race and destined to lead it. Russia helped him to arm and train his men and establish schools. The Tsaritsa of Russia herself founded a

Girls' School at Cetinje which was a centre of Pan-Slavism for the girls of Dalmatia and Bosnia and other parts of Turkey, and worked a great propaganda.

Nikola strove not only to develop the land within. He sought powerful alliances without. Most of all he aspired to be father-in-law to a Tsar of Russia and sent his eldest daughter to Petersburg with that hope. The poor girl, however, died there of tuberculosis, to which Montenegrins are peculiarly liable. The chance of ascending the throne of all the Russia's was lost, but the two succeeding Princesses formed Imperial alliances, Militza marrying the Grand Duke Petar and Anastasia becoming wife of the Grand Duke Nikola Nikolaievitch, recently so famous.

With his eye always on the throne of Serbia, Prince Nikola married his daughter Zorka to Petar Karageorgevitch, the then exiled pretender to the Serbian throne, who was Russia's protégé.

Being now strongly allied with the Slav Powers, he proceeded to connect his line with the Triple Entente. Prince Danilo, heir to the Princedom, married Militza, the daughter of the Grand Duke of Mecklenburg Strelitz. Princess Helena became Queen of Italy, and to make the claim to the Serbian throne doubly sure, the astute Prince Nikola married his second son, Mirko, to Natalie Constantinovitch, cousin to King Alexander of Serbia, who was then on the throne and who had no heir male. All that could be done by dynastic marriages for the greater glory of Montenegro was done. But it was to Russia that the Prince looked, and in Russia he and his people believed.

When I first visited the land in the early years of the present century, I found Russia spoken of as omnipotent and second only to God Almighty. The disaster of the Russo-Japanese war shook but did not shatter this faith.

In the 'seventies Nikola reached his zenith. Victoriously he led his armies against the Turks. All Europe applauded, recognised him as an independent Prince, and doubled the size of his Principality. Tennyson and Gladstone exalted him and his land. The future shone brightly. There was but one cloud in it. Prince Milan of Serbia, whom he despised, and who was the friend of Austria, was shortly raised to be King. The pro-Austrian Obrenovitches stood in the way of both Russia and Prince Nikola. This Pan-Slavism would not tolerate, and they were removed.

When Nikola, already well on in years, connived in 1903 at the assassination of King Alexander, it was with the full belief that it would lead him nearer his appointed goal. All Montenegro applauded the deed and cried: "Our Mirko will be King!" But another Tsar was on the throne and Nikola was not his "only friend". Russian policy had changed. Montenegro was too badly placed geographically to be a centre for Great Serbia. And Prince Nikola had erred fatally. He had tried to the best of his ability to be father to his country, his love for which was deep and indubitable. But like too many fathers, he had not reckoned on the pace at which children grow up. He clung to the *patria potestas* of former days. True, in 1905, he granted them a constitution and opened a Parliament. But it was on the lines of the old Soviet and had not real power. Fearing lest contact with the outer world should make his sons despise their stony heritage, he would not send them to a foreign university, and the two elder grew up with all the airs of royalty and none of the knowledge needed for a modern state, inadequately instructed at home by a Swiss tutor.

Similarly, education in the village schools was confined mainly to elementary facts learnt by heart and "histories" to inspire Great Serbian ideas. The press was most rigorously censored, and till very recently there was but one bookshop in the land, the wares of which were strictly supervised. But the days were past when a people could be brought up on ballads of the middle ages. Discipline and character training there was none. Those who learnt to read, battened on translations of the vilest French fiction imported by commercial travellers, and thought, alas, that they had achieved Western civilisation. Higher education there was none in Montenegro. Students went to Constantinople - not a nice place for boys - and to Belgrade to seek it.

Montenegro was thus far behind Serbia which for long years had benefited by the proximity of Vienna, one of the finest centres of culture in Europe. When war hate has calmed, it is to be hoped that Serbia will generously acknowledge her immense debt to Austria where all her best men were trained.

It was a very rude shock to Prince Nikola when he realised, as he very soon did, that Russia had thrown him over and that Petar Karageorgevitch was established on the Serbian throne as Russia's agent. Princess Zorka had long been dead, and between father-in-law and son-in-law no love was lost. Relations had long been strained, and after 1903 "the gloves were off". Prince Nikola, as old age approached, saw with pain that the prize for which he had devoted his life was eluding him, and made desperate efforts. They were vain.

Time had poured by in torrents since he mounted his

rocky throne. Old landmarks were swept away. But he and his had remained in the era in which they were born. Like all half-wild races, the Montenegrin is child-like and credulous, and at the same time crafty and cunning. Intrigue was the breath of old Nikola's nostrils. Just as one village family had planned and plotted against a neighbour, so had Nikola intrigued and plotted with Europe, but like many other Balkan politicians, he was apt to lose sight of the broader issues in a tangle of detail – a thing Abdul Hamid, whom Prince Nikola very much admired, rarely did.

Events hurried on. In 1907 Montenegro growled revolt, and a plot to assassinate Prince Nikola was formed by some Montenegrin students in Belgrade who came armed with Serbian bombs from the Royal arsenal. The plot failed. The Serbian Government denied knowledge of it, and refused either to make arrests or to extradite suspects. Prince Nikola believed Serbia incriminated, and the relations between the two States went from bad to worse. That poor Nikola was right was shown last November, when in the election programme of the radical party Radovitch, one of the conspirators, speaks of 1907 and sings the praise of Serbia "who protected our refugees, sustained our political champions, and instructed the youth of our nation". The rising generation forgot that Nikola had made Montenegro and obtained for it European recognition. And their ingratitude hurt the old man bitterly.

He made a last struggle. The annexation of Bosnia by Austria and the proclamation of Prince Ferdinand as Tsar of Bulgaria gave him, as the oldest Balkan ruler, a claim to Kingship. Europe consented, and at his Jubilee in 1910 he was proclaimed King. Ferdinand of Bulgaria was present at the celebrations. King Petar of Serbia was conspicuously absent. Relations between Montenegro and Bulgaria became close. Provided Ferdinand had the Bulgar districts of Macedonia, he was quite ready to see Nikola King of a Great Serbia. The arrangement in fact would have made far juster frontiers than the present ones.

With this in view, King Nikola and his army plunged into the first Balkan war of 1912 with enthusiasm, a fortnight before any other State, hoping and expecting to annex the coveted and disputed districts before Serbia took the field. And when, on the eve of battle, I, the only foreigner present, asked: "What about the Serb army?" I was told with shouts of laughter: "They are pig drovers!" We need not retell the disastrous result. In military knowledge and discipline, the Serb army hopelessly outpaced the Montenegrins and captured Prizren, the goal at which Nikola aimed.

It is a hard thing to end life as a failure. All that poor Nikola had lived for and worked for was gone. His sons had shown no military qualities and returned from camp despised by all. That either should ever ascend the throne, or keep it, seemed most doubtful. And the country threw the blame on their King. The poor old man, once the adored Gospodar of his people, remained, huge, powerful, puzzled, quite unable with his mediaeval outlook to wrestle with the insurgent twentieth century. He had meant so well, and in truth he was like a mastodon that by an odd chance had survived in a remote wilderness.

Before Montenegro could recover came the Great War in 1914. Montenegro recognised rightly, at once, that the Sarajevo murders meant that the final struggle for the construction of

Great Serbia had begun. Russia had thrown Nikola over. He believed that his death had been planned at Belgrade. The temptation was immense. Irresistible perhaps. Russian victory meant Karageorgevitch on the Great Serbian throne. A victory of the Central Powers, if he played his cards skilfully, might leave the Petrovitches as the good boys of the Serb people and their acknowledged head.

And it was the very last chance. The stakes lay there to his hand. All that was necessary was to come to terms with Austria. He did so, and withdrew from Montenegro in 1915 leaving Prince Mirko to keep the throne warm.

He played high – and he lost all. Nor can we utterly blame him. Had he succeeded, Jugo-Slavia could scarce have been in worse confusion than it is at present. And if he was an intriguer, what can we say of the Powers that played with him? Russia, his God, forsook him.

He worked for a high ideal – the liberation of a people. His faults were those of his race and his environment. His virtues were his own. He was picturesque, he was kindly, and he was courteous. He asked the peasant woman how her pigs were, and at Easter had red eggs in his breeches pockets for the tribesmen. He was brave, and, according to his lights, was very religious. Those of us who knew him can spare some moments of regret for the man who meant so well, but failed to cope with the rising tide of time, and has now died far from the grey mountains which he loved with all his heart.

[from: *The Contemporary Review,* London, Vol. 664, April 1921, p. 471-477.]

Albania:
The Oldest and Quaintest of Balkan Peoples

Throughout the western half of the Balkan peninsula—in Bosnia, Serbia, Montenegro, and Albania—the remains of a very early people are found in the prehistoric graves. They worked bronze skilfully and were among the earliest in Europe to work and use iron. Their origin is lost in the past.

About 600 B.C. they were invaded and probably largely influenced by the Celts, from the north. From this Celto-Illyrian stock the modern Albanian descends.

He is thus the oldest inhabitant of the Balkan peninsula, and the fact that he has survived the successive invasion and rule of the Romans, Bulgars, Serbs, and Turks, and remained Albanian, sufficiently proves his tenacious sense of nationality. No conqueror has succeeded in absorbing him Consequently, among the Albanians we still find traces of some of the earliest European customs.

Like the Scottish Highlanders, the Albanians were a tribal people. The tribes at an early date formed two groups, under separate princes. These groups we can still trace in the Ghegs

of the north and the
Tosks of the south. They are one and the same people, speaking the same Albanian tongue. The Ghegs, however, live in a far more rugged land, and in the natural fortresses of the mountains have retained some older usages than the Tosks of the south.

In the northern mountains the tribal system still holds its own, and in spite of oppressors and invaders, the tribesmen have ruled themselves by ancient unwritten law and customs, handed down from a remote period and administered by the elders of the tribe in solemn conclave.

The Northern Albanian has further shown his tenacity of purpose by the way large numbers of the tribesmen have remained faithful to the Roman Catholic Church. Albania was Christianised at a very early date. Scutari was a bishopric of the Patriarchate of Rome several centuries before the pagan Serbs and Bulgars were converted, and in spite of pressure brought to bear on them during the time that North Albania fell under Serb dominion in the Middle Ages, the North Albanians are among the very few of the Balkan peoples who consistently refused to join the Eastern Orthodox Church.

Each tribe has its patron saint and before the war, when the peasants were still well-to-do, they feasted this day magnificently, keeping "open house" to all neighbour co-religionists who crowded the small church to overflowing, knelt outside it in long lines, and when the service was over, ate sheep, roasted whole on long spits, until they could eat no more. The close-fitting white national dress of the men, braided heavily in black, their scarlet sashes and silver chains, the quaint black dresses of the women, their gay handkerchiefs and ornaments, made a picture that is unforgettable.

War has swept these lands and has left the starving population desolate, pillaged in turn by Montenegrin, Serb, Bulgar, and Austrian. But if given a chance by their predacious neighbours, the natural pluck and industry of the Albanian give reason to hope that in time he will rebuild his burnt villages and again raise big flocks on the rich mountain pastures; again crowd the bazaar of Scutari with livestock, cheese, and poultry, and have hides for export, and sumach to tan and dye them.

The townsman throughout Albania leads a very different life from his pastoral compatriot. He is usually a skilled craftsman and works industriously. Almost all the fine gold embroidery of the Balkans is Albanian work. The gorgeous Court dress of Montenegro was the creation of Albanian tailors. Most of the silversmiths of the Balkans, too, are Albanian or of Albanian descent. And, curiously enough, many of the designs still made by them resemble ornaments found in the prehistoric graves, so that both the skill and the pattern seem to be inherited from the ancient Illyrian.

In every town hand-weaving is extensively practised. Silk and cotton and woollen goods, often of beautiful and complicated design, are produced. As is usual in many Eastern lands, the town houses, as a rule, stand in their own garden or courtyard, which is surrounded by a high wall. The inhabitants live simply enough. There is little furniture, no stuffy hangings, whitewashed walls often re-whitened, a boarded floor often washed, and a gay carpet. The Albanian can set an example of cleanliness to many others.

Churches and mosques are both to be found in the larger towns. After the Turks had conquered Albania at the end of the fifteenth century, the Albanians for years prayed for the help of Christian Europe, and especially of Venice. None came, and in the eighteenth century Islam began to spread in Albania as in other Balkan lands. But the Albanian put race before religion, and both Christian and Moslem united to struggle against the Turks for independence. Nor is the Moslem Albanian fanatical. He often belongs to the very liberal Dervish sect of the Bektashis. Before the plundering of Albania during the recent wars, it was a pleasant sight to see the reverend Baba of a Bektashi monastery, with his great white cap and his silver earring, standing at the door distributing bread and alms to poor wayfarers.

Mixed marriages of Christian and Moslem took place in spite of the orders of the priests, and members of both religions can sometimes be found in one family. Very many of the tribes are mixed, and Christian and Moslem have the same national usages.

Old-world beliefs still lurk among the country folk. The fear of spells, magic, and the baleful evil eye haunts many a one. *Ore*, or spirits which flash like fire at night, are said to stop the traveller on his way, and the *shtriga*, or witchwoman, can make herself small like a fly, crawl through the keyhole, and suck her victim's blood. Perhaps the malaria-carrying mosquito is the origin of this belief. Folklore has usually some solid basis.

Though higher education is lacking, yet hereditary lore, handed down through generations, fills many gaps. There are peasants in Albania who can work cures of certain diseases and of simple disorders, and there may be met with native surgeons who are very skilful. They can perform operations, and they understand antiseptic treatment. Indeed, this seems to have been practised in Albania before it was known in England. Wounds were treated with *raki* instead of being washed with water as far back as any memory or record goes. A clever peasant surgeon will even mend a broken skull by replacing the bone by portions of ground shell.

Evil spirits are most active in March, and then mothers tie garlic round their children's necks to protect them. Mother has many other things to do also. She has to make the coarse maize bread, and bake it on the hearth under an iron cover upon which the hot wood-ash is piled. She saves the wood-ash carefully, and uses it in place of soap with which to wash the clothes, which come out beautifully clean. The maize is ground in primitive little water-mills with wooden turbine wheels, built over every torrent. Mother also weaves the thick woollen stuff and takes it to the fulling mill where two heavy wooden mallets, worked by waterpower, pound and beat it into a thick felt. And she plaits the black braid with which to trim it. The fire on the hearth seldom goes out. It is banked up at night. When the last male of a house dies, the women extinguish the fire as sign of mourning.

Rivers in some places are still crossed on inflated sheep skins or in big dug-out tree trunks.

Such has been country life. The reason it has been so primitive is because, under Turkish rule, the Albanians could only obtain any education by great difficulty and often risk.

The Albanian language, as spoken from the plains of Kosovo to the Gulf of Arta, has puzzled philologists. It is neither Greek nor Slav. It has a rather complicated Aryan grammar and has as its bedrock, doubtless, the tongue of the ancient Illyrian, the speech of Alexander the Great's Macedonian. For Strabo, writing in the first century A. D., tells us that both peoples spoke the same language. To this language the Albanian, whether Christian or Moslem, clings with an affection and tenacity which has something of the heroic.

In vain have Serb, Greek, and Turk tried to destroy it. Serb and Montenegrin have annexed thousands of Albanians and never permitted them to have a school or print a paper in their own tongue. The Christian Albanians of the south belong to the Eastern Orthodox Church, and here a Greek bishop once even excommunicated the Albanian language, and priests taught that it was useless to pray in Albanian, as Christ does not understand it.

The Turk punished with fifteen years' imprisonment anyone who taught the forbidden language or printed it, but the indomitable Albanian printed his books abroad and smuggled them in with difficulty and danger. He took advantage, too, of foreign aid. Italy and Austria, both intent on annexing Albania, started rival schools in the north, for propaganda purposes, with which the Turks dared not interfere. The Albanian learned—and remained Albanian. When he could afford it, he finished his education in Vienna or Paris. Many students were trained at Robert College by the Americans.

There have been martyrs to the national cause. But at length it has triumphed. The Albanian people have at last been granted independence in a part of the lands once theirs. Since the early part of 1920 they have been free to elect their own government and to reconstruct the land which, since 1914, has been overrun by seven armies. All Europe is reconstructing. Few lands with such slender resources have done more in the time to show a passionate desire to learn and to develop on national lines.

In two years no fewer than 528 schools have been opened. The towns have been cleaned up. Small hospitals have been opened. The post carries letters safely through the land. A smart gendarmerie has been organized. Public safety is ensured, and order reigns everywhere. Those of us who knew the land in Turkish days rub our eyes and can scarce believe them.

If enthusiasm were enough there could be no doubt of Albania's future. The will and the enthusiasm are there. The question is, what are Albania's resources? Her first and most pressing need is to have her frontiers recognized by the Powers, and so guaranteed that the country may be spared the constant drain and expense of defending them.

That done, Albania has much that can be developed. All the plain land, and much of the lower slopes of the hills, is highly fertile, and even with the present primitive implements and methods of cultivation, corn, maize, tobacco, the vine, and the olive flourish, as well as every kind of fruit and vegetable. Any capital sunk in draining the water-logged land at the mouths of the chief rivers would soon repay itself by increasing the arable land, and would also destroy the malaria which is bred in swamps. The mountain pastures are excellently adapted for sheep, goats, and cattle. But the thousands of beasts looted by the enemy need replacing. The breeding of a race of little horses, very good mountain climbers, with a dash of the Arab in them, was formerly one of Albania's assets. Here, again, war has deplenished the stock.

The mineral wealth of the land is not at present well investigated. There are copper and lignite near Scutari and Koritza. Asphalt has for many years been mined at Selenitza, near Valona, and petroleum is reported in the same district. Silk, linen, and hemp are grown and manufactured in small quantities for local use. Scutari has a small export of caviar and dried fish.

Lastly, Albania has her magnificent mountain scenery as beautiful as any in Europe, and as yet unexploited, and awaiting the traveller who does not mind roughing it a bit and finds a pleasure in the unbeaten track. There are mountains to be climbed known as yet only to the herdsman. There are trout in the mountain streams, snipe and woodcock in the marshes, and wild boar in the forests. The Albanian Alps only need to be known to become one of the "playgrounds of Europe."

[from: J. A. Hammerton, ed. *Peoples of all Nations*, London, 1922, p. 46-60.]

A Bird Tradition
in the West of the Balkan Peninsula

The fact that a considerable proportion of the people of the Western side of the Balkan peninsula even to-day identify themselves with birds, and that a mass of traditional songs shows that the belief is ancient, has not, so far as I know, received the notice it deserves. Briefly the facts are as follows.

The Albanians in their own language call themselves Shkypetars, their language Shkyp, and their land Shkyperia or Shkypnia. They derive this from "Shkyp," an eagle, and say, "we are the sons of the eagle, our land is the land of eagles." Beyond a vague idea that to kill an eagle is unlucky I have learnt no particulars. But in Plutarch's "Life of Pyrrhus, King of Epirus," who is still a popular hero in Albania, it is of interest to find that after his great victory over the Macedonians, his Epirots hailed him as the "Eagle." The mediaeval chieftain Skenderbeg adopted an eagle for his banner, and the eagle has been chosen as the crest of the newly-formed Albanian State.

Passing from Albania into Montenegro (now merged in Jugoslavia), I found a very strongly marked tradition. As all maps up to the end of the eighteenth century, and indeed into the nineteenth, merely mark Montenegro as a part of North Albania, and as much of the tribal law and custom was the same in both lands till 1865, it is not surprising to find that all Montenegrins also are birds. But, in this case, falcons (*soko*, pl. *sokolovi*). This word is used in common parlance. When I tramped the country my guide hailed everyone we met on the way with "Whither will ye, my falcons?" or, "Forward, my falcons!" (*napried sokolevi*), and so forth. Every officer addressed his men as "*Moji sokolovi*" (my falcons). I have heard this again and again. There is also a verb derived from "*soko*," "*sokoliti*," to urge on, or incite. *Soko, Sokol,* and the derivatives *Sokolitch* and *Sokolovitch* are common enough names among the South Slavs.

The Montenegrins have a dance which seems to be unknown in Serbia. A pair or two pair of dancers stand opposite each other and dance at each other, retiring, advancing and performing various steps and finally leaping as high as possible into the air, flapping their arms and uttering wild yells. The leaping, flapping, yelling dancer is said to represent a falcon or eagle. When danced at night by a big bonfire it is extraordinarily picturesque. I once saw this danced by a North Albanian tribesman, and was told it was Albanian. But the Albanian tribesmen very rarely dance, whereas the Montenegrins seldom lost a chance of doing so.

The custom of death wailing was universal when I was in Montenegro. In these wails a large number of stock phrases are used, interspersed with howls and shrieks of "Lé lé lé lé!" The men of the tribe when approaching the house of the deceased cried:

*"Zhao ni za tebe
Moj' krilati brate!"*
(Woe is me for thee, oh my winged brother.)

I could get no explanation of the word "winged" except that "we always say it," or "it is our custom," and at first supposed it meant an angel. But taken along with the other facts, it probably indicates that the man was a "soko," and also, as we shall see later, a brave man entitled to wear plumes.

The use of the word *soko* for a fighting man is so common in Montenegrin songs that I could easily fill a page with quotations. Grand Voyvoda Mirko, father of the late King Nikola of Montenegro, a wild man of the mountains, whose life was occupied alternately with border fighting and composing ballads on his frays, supplies any number of examples in his *Junachki Spomenik* (Heroes' Monument), dealing with the fights between 1852 and 1862. "Voyvoda Jovo was drinking wine in his tower at Banyani. With the Voyvoda were three hundred falcons. Among them, two grey falcons, both heroes, Sirdar Stepan Radoyev and Sirdar Djoko of Banyani." In "The Avenging of Pope Radosav," the Kapetan cries that he has news from Biyelopavlitch "that the Turks have broken faith and killed that grey falcon Pope Radosav... Now up with ye, my falcons, let us go and avenge him, etc." Briefly, almost everyone is a falcon, and the leaders urge on (*sokoliti*) their men. The thing becomes comical when we are told "three grey falcons sat drinking wine before the inn." The names of three chieftains are then given. I have heard a love song yelled: "Thou art the swallow bird— I am the grey falcon who will swoop and carry you off." Whether this song was old or new I do not know.

The use of the term "*soko*" to denote a warrior is very much more frequent in the ballads of Montenegro than in those of Serbia (in the pre-War sense). Thus in those concerning the Serb rising led by Karageorge at the beginning of the nineteenth century, I have found scarcely an example.

Turning to the old ballads, of which large numbers have been collected and published, we find many curious facts about falcons. Falcons carry special messages to Serb chieftains. Want of space prevents quoting these tales in entirety, though many well deserve it. In "The Sons of Ivan Beg" (about 1510) given in *Ogledalo Srpsko*, the chief Montenegrin collection of traditional ballads, Ivan Tsrnoievitch, Prince of Montenegro, drinks wine at Cattaro with some comrades. A grey falcon hovers over the market-place. The Montenegrins try to hunt it into a corner and catch it, but it soars aloft. Ivan then wraps his cloak around his shoulders and calls to the falcon, which settles on his shoulder and gives him a letter from under its wing which it has brought him from Stamboul. Ivan addresses it as "My falcon, thou black news carrier." And they have a long talk about Ivan's renegade son Stanisha.

The falcon as influencing the fate of the Serb nation appears in one of the Kosovo cycle songs (see collection of Vuk Karadjitch) thus: "A falcon, that grey bird, flew from Holy Jerusalem and carried a little swallow. This was not a grey falcon, but holy St. Elijah. He did not carry a swallow, but a letter from the Holy Mother of God." This letter tells King Lazar how, by losing the coming battle of Kosovo (1389), he may save his own soul. Which he accordingly does! Among the songs about that most popular hero, Marko Kralyevitch, are some references of much interest. Marko, of course, is often referred to as a falcon.

He is described as winning a shooting competition against the Turks by using an arrow fledged with six falcon feathers. Two songs describe the love that exists between him and falcons, "Kralyevitch Marko fell sorely ill by the wayside. He thrust his spear in the ground and tied his horse Sharatz to it. And Marko cried aloud: 'Who will bring me water to drink? Who will make shade for me?' Down there came a grey falcon, and brought water in its beak, and spread its wings over him... And Marko said: 'Oh falcon, my grey bird, what good have I done thee that thou shouldst bring water and make shade for me?' And the falcon said: 'Don't be silly, Marko! When we were in the fight at Kosovo, the Turks took me and cut off both my wings. Then didst thou take me and set me up on a green fir tree that the Turkish horses might not trample me, and fed'st me with the flesh of heroes, and gave me blood to drink. Thus hast thou done me a good deed.'" In a longer version the bird is an eagle. Marko rescues it from the battle, and also saves its nestlings from a burning tower, and feeds them "for a month and one week more." In a third song, Marko goes a-hunting with the Turks, and his falcon when flying at a duck is shot by a Turk with an arrow, and falls with a broken wing. In barbarous times, bloody vengeance for a favourite horse or hound is not impossible. But Marko's conversations with his falcon seem to show a more intimate relation. The wounded bird settled on Marko's shoulder and cried ceaselessly. Marko riding home with it asks: "How art thou, my falcon, without a wing?" and the falcon said: "I am like one that has no brother. Had I a born brother, I would not lament my wing, for he would avenge me." And Marko said: "Fear not, my grey falcon. An thou hast no brother, thou hast Marko, who will be no worse than a brother to thee." Marko arrives home and sends for a doctor, who dresses the falcon's wound. News comes that seventy Turks have been harassing a neighbouring village. Marko, single-handed, kills everyone of them and returning home remarks: "Now fear not, my falcon. Thou knowest thou hast a brother. So long as Marko lives, the Turks will never forget thy wing." Marko was an historical personage (end of fourteenth century), son of Vukashin, chieftain of Scutari, in Albania, when that district fell under Serbian rule. That is, he hails from the very district where the falcon legend still prevails.

In one ballad, "Childe Jovan and the Daughter of Tsar Stefan," we seem to have a reminiscence of actual descent from a falcon. The local colour is mediaeval Serbian. Tsar Stefan of Prizren must be Stefan Dushan, who reigned from 1336-1350. But the tale is obviously an ancient one tacked on to a later celebrity. Briefly, the Tsar's daughter is found to be pregnant. Charged by her father, she confesses. According to custom she lives shut up in a sort of harem. "One morning I arose early... I went out on to the white tower and put the crown upon my head, to see how it suited me, until the sun rose in the east. When the crown saw the sun, beams of light flashed from the crown... as far as the Shar Mountains where the falcons nest. And the beautiful *Vilas* (fairies, spirits) are with them... When night came ... a grey falcon came flying, and with him seven swans from the Shar Mountains and Jastreb. The swans alighted on the tower, the falcon upon my window sill. The tower shook. Light streamed forth from the falcon so that my golden cage (harem) was light at midnight as at midday. The falcon shook its wings and stood there a youth in a thin shirt. He stayed the whole night, and left early at morn. Never again has he returned to me, and by him am I with child." The Tsar drives out his daughter, and she seeks her lover. She is guided partly by the sun. By the help of his old mother, she finds the tower of her falcon lover, and upon it is a golden ball with falcons' wings (Is this a trace of Egyptian cults?). His mother, to prevent her son from again flying away, steals his falcons' feathers while he sleeps, and he is in consequence killed by the jealous *Vilas*, who will not permit him to have a human wife.

Has this tale of a falcon and the sun any remote connection with the bird chariot of the sun found in Bosnia? Has it been handed down from prehistoric times to the now completely Slavised population? The tale is evidently fragmentary, for we are never told whether the falcon's child is born.

In the two versions of another tale: "Sekula Changes Himself to a Dragon" (Vuk Karadjitch Collection, Vol. 2, p. 498), we find an actual statement of relationship to the falcon. The tale purports to be an account of the second battle of Kosovo, that fought by Janos Huniades against the Turks on 17th-19th October, 1448. Knolles, writing in 1620, says: "Zekell Huniades, his sister's son, was the first of the leaders there slain in the thickest of the Turkes." The ballad clothes this historical fact in a myth. Huniades figures in Serb ballads as Sibinja Yanko (John of Sibinj, or Hermannstadt, in Transylvania, of which he was Voyvoda). Yanko makes ready to ride to Kosovo, and takes with him his sister's only son—young Sekula—in spite of the urgent remonstrances of his sisters and his mother. The maidens of various places they ride through foretell Sekula's death, and beg him to stay with them, in vain. When they reached Kosovo plain, they spread their tents and Voyvoda Yanko said: "Up with ye, my falcons! Keep guard against the Turks while I sleep a while." Sekula said to Yanko: "Oh, uncle, (*ujko* — mother's brother), go thou now and sleep a while. I will steal to the Turkish camp and change myself to a six-winged dragon, and will bring thee the mighty Sultan in my teeth in the form of a falcon. When thou risest up from sleep, oh uncle, do not let reason give way to madness! Shoot not the six-winged dragon, but shoot the grey falcon." Yanko slept, and Sekula stole to the Turkish camp, changed himself to a dragon, and duly alighted on Yanko's tent with the Sultan in his teeth in the form of a grey falcon. All the warriors roared at once: "In an evil hour hast thou lain down, oh Voyvoda Yanko, and in a worse hast arisen." Yanko leapt to his feet and seized a golden arrow. He thought, and thought at once: "Why should I shoot the grey falcon, for I am myself a falcon, and of the race of falcons. Better that I shoot the six-winged dragon." He shot an arrow from his golden bow, and shot the six-winged dragon. It hissed and loosed the falcon. The falcon arose to the clouds and flew to the Turkish camp. The dragon fell to the ground. Voyvoda Yanko hissed for rage, and his sister's son Sekula said to him: "Oh, Uncle Yanko, did I not tell thee not to change reason for madness — that thou shouldst not shoot the six-winged dragon but shoot the grey falcon?" Sekula dies of his wound, and the tale ends.

The fact that Sibinja Yanko, who was not a Serb but a Vlach, should claim kinship with the falcon is at first puzzling. But the fragments of a much more elaborate version explain it. In this version, when Yanko awoke and saw the dragon on his tent he called to George Ban Despot (the Brankovitch), who was then Prince of the Serbs under Turkish suzerainty: "Oh, my brother in God, George Ban Despot, dost see the great marvel upon my white tent? A six-winged dragon hath seized a grey falcon. The falcon is hissing like a serpent. Shall I kill the dragon or the falcon?" And George Ban Despot said to Yanko of Sibinja: "Are we not of the brood of falcons, and the Turks are a brood of dragons? Strike the dragon, do not strike the falcon." Yanko shoots three arrows. The dragon only looses the falcon when mortally wounded by the third arrow. Sekula, dying, upbraids his uncle as in the former version. This version is in all probability the original one. For here it is the Serb, George Brankovitch, who claims kinship with the falcon, and obtains the liberation of the Sultan. Historic truth lurks beneath the allegory, for George betrayed Huniades, and so led to his defeat at Kosovo.

That eagle plumes were actually recently worn as a mark of heroism is shown by the following account taken from *Les Quatres Premiers Livres de Navigations et Pérégrinations de Nicholas de Nicholay*, 1568. He was French Ambassador to the Sultan, and gives a detailed account of the many types of people he came across, with elaborate drawings. Among them one of a Deli (= brave fool, crazy warrior). These formed part of the retinue of the Pashas and Begs, and were, in fact, the Bashibazouks of those days. "These," he says, "are adventurers who follow the Turkish army voluntarily and without payment, except that they are fed and kept at the expense of the Bashas, etc., who have each a number in his suite. These fellows are inhabitants of Bosnia and Serbia... The first I saw was at Adrianople. His coat and large breeches were of the skin of a bear with the fur outside. On his head he wore a bonnet... hanging over one shoulder, made of a leopard skin well spotted, and in front of it, to make him look the more furious, he had fastened the great tail of an eagle. And its two wings were fastened with gilt nails to his targe, which he wore slung at his side. I was curious as to his country and religion. He said he was of the Serbian nation, and as to his religion, he was now living with the Turks and so dissimulated, but by birth and heart he was a Christian... I asked why he went so strangely clad, and he said it was to make himself look the more furious to his enemies. As for the plumes, none might wear them but such as gave proof of valour. For among them these plumes were esteemed as the true ornament of a valiant man of war.

Nicholay's description is confirmed by one of the ballads of the celebrated Heyduk, Old Man Novak, who carried on the profession of brigandage with great éclat at about the end of the fifteenth century, in Bosnia. In the "Marriage of Gruitz Novakovitch" (Vuk Karadjitch Collection, Vol. 3), Old Man Novak, when going out to fight the Greek whose bride he has snatched for his son Gruitz, dresses himself "in terrible clothing" made of a bear's skin. A wolf's head with an eagle's wing in it forms his cap, and his eyebrows are made of owl's feathers.

Another celebrated chieftain, Relja, who ruled the Novipazar district, and is said to have died about 1343, is known in the ballads and in national tradition as Relja Krilatitza—Relja the winged bird, or as Relja Krilati, winged Relja. Thus, in "The Sister of Lek Kapetan" (Karadjitch, Vol. 2) "now shalt thou behold a beautiful bridegroom, Winged Relja! A winged warrior is no joke!"

In a great number of songs the various heroes are described as wearing fur caps, with silver plumes called *chelenka* in them. These are described as being given as rewards of valour, some wearing ten or a dozen. A few specimens of these old *chelenka* are in the Sarajevo Museum. I give sketches of two. They have coloured stones set in them, which at first sight suggest peacocks' feathers. Nevertheless they may, I think, be taken as a stylised wing and tail.

The bodyguard of the late king of Montenegro was formed of picked men who were known as Perianitzi, from *perianik*, a plume wearer. I was told that until recent years these men wore eagles' feathers in their caps.

I possess a Montenegrin *gusle* (musical instrument) carved by a peasant of Nyegushi as lately as 1902. Its head is formed by a grotesque carving of Milosh Obilitch, who killed Sultan Murad in 1389. On Milosh's cap sits a dicky bird, which, I was told, represents the *sivi soko*, and indicates that Milosh was *dobar junak* (a great hero). It is a far cry from the prehistoric bird-chariot of Bosnia to my Montenegrin *gusle*. And it would be rash to say that they have any connection. But that a form of bird cult has existed continuously for a very long period on the western side of the Balkan peninsula seems clear.

The very recently formed gymnastic clubs of the Czechs, which have been the most popular and efficient form of nationalist propaganda, are called Sokels, and the members wear a falcon's feather in their caps. But whether the Czechs have a falcon tradition of their own, or if they adopted the term from their Slav neighbours further south, I have not been able to ascertain.

[from: *Man, Journal of the Royal Anthropological Society*, London, April 1923, p. 55-61.]

Head-Hunting in the Balkans

Head-hunting, studied usually in distant lands, flourished in Europe well into the middle of the 19th century and is not yet quite extinct. When I travelled in Montenegro at the beginning of the present century all the elderly men could, and did, tell tales of the heads that they or their friends had taken. My guide confessed, with shame and humiliation, that he had not taken a single one in the war of 1877, pleading that he was only seventeen, and was severely told that others, even younger, had done better.

Every man in earlier days went to war or to a border fray intending to take as many heads as he could. The short heavy "hanzhar" was used for the purpose. Never for stabbing. An expert severed the head at one blow. If two Montenegrins both wounded the same man, the head "legally" belonged to the man who took first blood. I was told of cases in which a dispute followed about the head and that the rival claimants have been known to fight each other for it to the death. The reasons for head-taking were given as "to show how brave you are" and "to shame the enemy." I gathered that it was also supposed to affect the future life of the enemy. But whether it would prevent it altogether I could not learn. That it was formerly believed to do so seems probable, as I heard grisly tales of heroic women who crawled over the border at night and, with danger and difficulty, brought back their husbands' heads in order to bury them with the bodies.

Blood vengeance raged between Montenegrin, Turk and Albanian, and for one head many would be taken. The heads were tied by the lock of hair left on them to the neck or belt of the warrior. A Ragusan lady gave me her grandfather's vivid account of the horror produced there when the Russians enlisted Montenegrins to fight the French troops during the Napoleonic wars, and how the wild inrush of yelling Montenegrins, with decapitated French heads dripping and dangling from belt and neck, struck terror into Napoleon's hardened troops.

Till recently the heads of all Serbs, Montenegrins and Albanians were shaven and a long lock, plait, or two side tufts only left. The reason popularly given for this custom was that if the head was completely shaven the only way to carry it was by hooking your finger in its mouth. If you were a Christian, you would not like a Moslem finger stuck in. Nor would a Moslem like an unclean Christian finger. Hence a handle was left. The reason is improbable, but the tale is of interest as showing that a large proportion of the people were accustomed to the idea of having their heads carried away!

The mediaeval ballads of the Serbs give plenty of examples of head-cutting and narrate mainly the slaying of chieftains by chieftains. To realise the wholesale head-taking of recent times we must refer to the ballads of Grand Voyvoda Mirko, father of the late King of Montenegro, who gives very precise details.

Thus, in "The Slaying of Chulek Beg," 1852, after the fight, they "counted out three hundred Turkish heads. Among them that of Chulek Beg... Off went the Serbs singing and carrying Turkish turbans and glittering clothing and the Turkish heads on oaken stakes and Chulek's head among them."

In the fight at Drobnjak, 1855, "As the Turks rushed from the burning tower, the young Montenegrins seized them and cut off the head of each. And lo and behold the three Mladitches, carrying dead Turkish heads... and they said to Serdar Bogdan of the frontier 'Here, oh Serdar, have we cut off for thee fifty Turkish heads and taken all their clothing.'"

In the "Slaying of Betchko Agimanitch" to avenge one Montenegrin, twelve Turks are killed. "Then with the Turks' clothes and weapons and the heads upon oaken stakes they marched back to the village of Markovitch and set up eleven heads before the white tower of the Serdar, and Betchko's head they carried to Cetinje to the tower above the Monastery where up till now many Turkish heads have been impaled and a many more shall be, God willing, heads of Pashas and Vizirs, of Agas and Begs... A fine booty was this of Serdar Scepan and great honour did he gain. God grant him long life!"

Sir Gardner Wilkinson, who went as British Envoy to Montenegro in 1848, broke it gently to Prince Nikola (as he then was) that the sight of so many heads on a tower in the capital was unpleasant to British envoys. But the practice continued and a dried head was kept in the Monastery after public exhibition had ceased.

In "The Avenging of Pope Radisav" we find thirty-three heads taken to avenge one man. "They cut off thirty-three heads. Not the devil a one did they let live... And they went to Bijelopavlitch, above the bloody town of Spuzh [then in Turkish possession], carrying the heads on stakes, and stuck them up that the Turkish wives and women of the town might see them and know they were a monument to Pope Radisav. May the ravens and crows claw the heads and the foxes tear them!"

These were border frays. More serious work was put in at Kolashin in 1858. Here, 1,000 heads were cut off. "I was on Kum mountain and I saw it myself," adds the poet proudly. In the "Slaying of Selim Pasha" in 1862, 1,600 heads are taken, including those of the Pasha and his two sons, and carried in triumph. In the fight at Nikshitch the same year the score is 3,700. It is noteworthy that a share of the booty, some fine swords or horses, were usually sent to the Prince (the late King of Montenegro) after every big affair. That the heads were cut from dead bodies and from the wounded is shown by "The Fight of Martinitch," 1862: "By the time they had driven the Turks back on Spuzh they had cut off 600 heads, and mortally wounded 1,000 men whom the Turks carried away that the Serbs might not cut off their heads too."

The last heads that I heard of as being cut off were those of three Montenegrins killed in a border fight just preparatory to the first Balkan war in August, 1912. I spoke with a nephew of one of the decapitated. He took it very calmly and seemed to think it might happen to anybody's uncle. During the war which followed, nose-taking was substituted by the Montenegrins for head-taking and a great deal went on. I saw nine of the victims. The nasal bone was hacked right through and the whole upper lip removed as well as the nose. The trophy was carried by the moustache. It is only fair to the Turks to say that I did not see or hear of a single case of a mutilated Montenegrin. The practice was to go round the battle-field and cut the nose, and in some cases also castrate, the wounded, who usually died of the additional shock and haemorrhage.

The desire to take a trophy was so great that a wounded Montenegrin whose hands were disabled would sometimes seize his enemy's nose with his teeth and try to bite it off. A Montenegrin gendarme told me how, in the war of 1877, he had thus made a supreme effort, had been cut down, and on recovering consciousness in a Russian field hospital found, to his intense joy, the nose in his breeches pocket, a friend having generously cut it off for him!

I once stopped a terrible fight on the road between Cattaro and Njegus, in which one man had his teeth firmly fixed in the other's nose and was hanging on like a bulldog, while the blood dripped freely from the ends of his enemy's long moustache.

Turning to the best collection of old Montenegrin ballads, *Ogledalo Srpsko*, we find many more examples of head-taking, and further confirmation of the fact that the dead heads were worn by the triumphant victors. Thus in "The Slaying of Bechir Beg Bushatli," "the Krajitchnitzi, those grey falcons, charged down on the rest of the Turks and cut off fifty heads... They then turned back towards home decked out with Turkish heads and many Turkish weapons... and they carried the heads to Cetinje and ornamented Cetinje with them." This in 1839. In the case of mighty Pashas I was told it was sometimes customary to salt the head to make it keep the longer.

I could multiply instances, but have given sufficient to

show the ardour with which head-hunting was pursued in Europe, within five days of London, during the lifetime of many of us.

[from: *Man, Journal of the Royal Anthropological Society,* London, February 1923, p. 19-21.]

The Balkans as a Danger Point

The Near East has been the cause of more war, quarrel, and intrigue between the Great Powers than perhaps any other spot in Europe. "Why are all the Great Powers building palaces to hold their Legations in Cetinje, which is a mere mountain village?" I asked the Italian architect who was building the Russian Legation house there in 1900. He very truthfully replied: "Because Montenegro is the matchbox upon which the next European war will be lighted." The whole Balkan Peninsula is a matchbox, and not a safety one. The Near Eastern question is asked in some five languages understood by few in the West, and asked by people so far removed in mentality from these of the West that neither party can understand the other.

There are two Balkan problems: the internal, and the external.

Within the Peninsula four separate nations—Greek, Serb, Bulgar, and Albanian—each put forth claims which cannot all be satisfied at once. Each has an arguable case. In turn each has had a "glorious past" and swayed wide lands, and wishes to revive that past, despite the fact that all conditions are changed.

I pointed out to a Balkan schoolmaster that the Middle Ages cannot be revived and that certain Serb claims are now as unjustifiable as would be England's claim to North France. He replied contemptuously: "You have a navy. Why do you not go and take it?"

Each Balkan nation has for centuries taught its children that the other was its hereditary foe. So deep-seated were, and are, these hatreds that till 1912 each Balkan race has sided with the Turk against his rival. Had the Bulgar and the Serb risen in 1897 when the Greek did, the Turk could have been driven from Macedonia. Had the Greek aided the Bulgar revolt in 1903, success might have been obtained. But, as several bishops then declared to me: "Better the Turk should remain here for ever than that the Greek [or Bulgar, as the case might be] should gain one kilometre." And when after some five centuries of Turk rule the Balkan nations made an alliance in 1912 it lasted a bare six months.

These internecine quarrels of the Balkan peoples are not in themselves a danger to Europe. They balanced each other, helped keep the Turk in Europe and maintained things *in statu quo*. They became dangerous only because each Balkan nation in order to beat his hated rival has allowed himself to become the tool of one or more Great Powers, each of which worked for its own ends and cared nothing for the fate of the tool. Few things are more despicable than the way the Great Powers have posed hypocritically as champions of oppressed Christians; have surreptitiously helped those same Christians to destroy each other, and have incited each to rise against the Turk solely in order to obtain for themselves the right to exploit the Balkan Peninsula.

The Balkan Peninsula is one of the few unexploited corners of Europe; fertile, well watered, possessing unworked mineral wealth, and possibly oil. Any Great Power will rush to save Christians or reform the administration of a land possessing oil. The Peninsula is also one of the most important strategical points of Europe; the gate between Europe and Asia. So strongly have the Powers realised this that they too, like the small Ba'kan nations, have refrained from evicting the Turk lest a hated rival should profit thereby. None wished to pull chestnuts from the fire for its neighbour.

The Balkan problem, we must not forget, is not which town shall be Serb and which Greek, etc., *but which European race shall eventually hold the gate of Europe and Asia and control Europe's destiny.*

Such being the internal and external Balkan problems, is there any distinct march of events in the past which may indicate the future? In the past forty years archaeology has illumined much that before was dim. We have evidence of great mass movements. Through long ages the peoples of Europe have been pressed steadily from east to west till in historic times they have been forced across the Atlantic. There seems to be no return ticket on the journey from east to west any more than when we "go West" altogether.

What are these human tides that sweep westward? Certain human types are found in certain districts. In historical times they grouped themselves into what we now call nations or Powers. But each such nation is in continual flux, absorbing new or losing old elements. Nature never stands still. There is either growth or decline. No frontiers can last much longer than the generation of the men that drew them. But statesmen have learnt nothing from the example of King Canute and still howl when the tide flows over their boots.

There are three main racial elements in Europe: the long-skulled, short, dark, folk of the Mediterranean basin, common to the whole Mediterranean coast; the Nordic race, equally long-skulled but taller and fairer—the Anglo-Saxon, Norman, Dane, Scandinavian, North German—forming too a large part of our own population and part of that of North France; and the broad, short-skulled people, by far the largest race numerically, with which the Nordic mixes to the east and the south. The latter occupy a vast area extending from, and including, Russia and reaching thence to the Pyrenees by way of Poland, Czecho-Slovakia, Bavaria, Wurtemburg, most of Switzerland, Alsace-Lorraine, Savoy, and the Auvergne. East of Russia, the short-skulled people extend to the Pacific. Archaeology and history alike show that these short-skulled people have been and are crowding out the long-skulled. Prehistoric graves in lands which are now short-skulled yield skulls as long as those of the purest Anglo-Saxon and German type (save only in lands which are very mountainous and were probably uninhabited by another race when the short-skulled folk arrived). Only in England was the short-skulled man completely absorbed by the indigenous long-skulled population. He left a characteristic culture, but his skull only as that of a dead man.

It would appear that the short-skulled folk permeated Europe by trekking slowly in great family groups, urged on probably by famine in the steppes or the pressure of tribes east of them. To this day they can live under far harder circumstances than the long-skulled folk and in prehistoric days they settled mainly along the mountains of Central Europe.

When at the beginning of the Christian era the Teutonic tribes flooded south and west into the Roman Empire, another march of the short-skulled people took place. The Slavonic peoples trekked in from east to west, flooding Central Europe. It was their movement probably which drove the Teuton west and south; modern Saxony is largely short-skulled. The Anglo-Saxon was hunted westward to our island.

The Teutonic Emperor Charles the Great checked the Slav thrust in the ninth century, and the long struggle between the Teuton and the Slav began. The Teuton in a struggle of centuries checked the Slav and dominated him, but failed to evict him. But the Teutonic wedge driven down south as far as Vienna, saved Western Europe from the Slav flood.

Another broad-skulled man, the Magyar, poured in from east to west and separated the North and South Slavs. Meanwhile in the seventh century the Slavs had flooded the Balkan Peninsula, where a largely short-skulled people was already in possession and the old long-skulled Greek was hunted even into the Morea. On the top of this Slav invasion came another east to west short-skulled invader— the Turk.

Every invasion so far has reinforced the short-skulled mass. Our own, the long-skulled man, has never been reinforced and dwindles steadily in Europe. Has he had his day in Europe and is that of the short-skulled man dawning? That is now the meaning of the Near Eastern question. Two great civilisations, one developing from the other, that of the Mediterranean peoples and that of the Nordic, have so far moulded and influenced not only Europe but a large part of the world. In recent times an unprecedented flood of scientific discovery and mechanical invention has changed the earth's surface.

As yet the Slav has profited by the inventions of others, but has not originated any. His influence has been rather destructive than constructive. He has penetrated many lands as cheap labour. He can undersell the luxury-loving, long-skulled man and yet live in what to him is luxury. And often he has played the part of anarchist and revolutionary in the lands to which he has emigrated. As an odd coincidence we find a long line of religious heresies running from Asia Minor to the Pyrenees along the short-skulled line—Manicheans, Bogomili, Hussites, Waldenses and Albigenses. Retzius, the Swedish anthropologist, writing in 1909 of the advance of the short-skulled people, said: "The prospect is depressing, it cannot be denied. But the development of things in the world is not seldom harsh and unmerciful." Since he wrote this, things have made a startling stride. We ourselves have helped tear down the one barrier, the Teuton, which stood before the oncoming Slav, and the Slav now regards Europe as lying at his feet. The whole Slav mass has been put into a position of power it could not have attained unaided for many centuries. "We made you destroy the Austrian and German Empires for us," said a Serb lately; "now, so soon as Russia is ready, the Slav people will fulfil their destiny. You cannot stop us." The Serb has contempt for us: "You English are so stupid. You are not *rusé*. Anyone can cheat you!" "We do not want English culture," was the reason lately given in Serbia for imprisoning a harmless English tourist.

For the first time for centuries, one race—the Serb—dominates the Balkan Peninsula, and that race the chosen ally of Russia. The Slav people as a whole, as all who have lived among them know, believe that it is their destiny to rule Europe and carry to it their culture. And of this destiny Russia regarded herself as the Heaven-sent agent. Russia is just how passing through a fever. But there is nothing to indicate that her objective will be changed. Formerly it was her "mission" to spread her Holy Orthodox Church, now she intends to spread her wholly unorthodox forms of government and economics over Europe. A change in name only. Sooner or later Russia will again press westward and find stronger tools than before to her hand.

The *Livre Noir*[iii] and Von Siebert's book[iv] throw great light on Russia's pre-war diplomacy in France and England. France dazzled with the idea of obtaining Alsace-Lorraine, financed Russia to an enormous extent. Then, when Russia had decided on using Serbia as a tool, France in 1906 obligingly began to finance and arm Serbia, too. We then began military conversations with France and, as Serbia formed part of Russia's (and France's) war schemes, we had to resume the diplomatic relations with Serbia which we dropped when King Alexander was murdered. The murderers themselves were needed as officers later on.

Russia had formerly meant to use Bulgaria as a land bridge to Constantinople, but finding that Bulgaria meant to be independent, Russia cast her aside cynically. Montenegro, Russia's faithful dog for centuries, was also marked down for destruction. Russia, like Juggernaut, crushes all worshippers relentlessly beneath her chariot wheels in fulfilment of her "divine mission." When the Anglo-Entente with Russia was made, the Russian colony at Cetinje, which had been markedly

---

iii *Un Livre Noir: Diplomatie d'avant-guerre, d'après les documents des archives russes.* 2 volumes.

iv *Diplomatische Aktenstücke zur Geschichte der Ententepolitik der Vorkriegsjahre.* 3 volumes.

cold, received me with wild enthusiasm. "Russia" they told me, "is God's agent. You have stood in our path till now. Now the way is clear. We shall fight Germany together."

Russia regarded all her allies as mere tools. We were to get nothing out of the deal but the blessings of the Holy Orthodox Church. Benckendorff's despatches from London show what he and his Government thought of us. Thus on February 19th, 1914, he writes in reply to Sazonoff, who is anxious to tighten the Entente into a defensive alliance:

"In England ... they find it convenient to leave Grey to do as he likes with scarce a question. There is good as well as inconvenience in this. Were it possible to force matters, it would be a bad job... for the opposition would arise and neutralise the results which you and Grey pursue. In spite of appearances, Grey is constantly anxious about the threat of German hegemony... You must not hustle him... Repeated reproaches will certainly annoy him... Is not the true difference between the Triple Alliance and the Triple Entente that, whereas the Triple Alliance is formed of three Powers with equal rights, the Triple Entente is formed of a master and two acolytes whom the master permits to act or restrains till the moment comes to give commands?... Simply to administer mustard to Grey seems to me doubtful therapy."

This is how Russia saw us. An acolyte, whose Foreign Minister was to be played gently—above all no mustard! Of France, the other acolyte, he writes yet more cynically on February 25th, 1913:

"M. Cambon and I are on confidential terms, perhaps unique between Ambassadors. He shows me nearly everything. Much more than I show him... Of all the Powers, France is the one which would accept war most philosophically. France, as has been said, 'has recovered herself.' Rightly or wrongly she has complete faith in her army. The old ferment of hatred is working and she might think present circumstances [the Balkan wars] more favourable than they would be later... It must not happen that war breaks out *on account of interests more French than Russian*; above all, not in circumstances which might be more favourable to France than to Russia."[v]

France, in fact, was to pay the Russian piper, and the piper was to call the tune. The archives show meanwhile how Russia, with Hartwig as Minister at Belgrade, built up her Balkan policy by forming the Balkan alliance which was to set the ball rolling when Russia was ready, and result in the fulfilment of her "divine and historic mission." The plan was nearly wrecked by the Balkan people rushing to war on their own account in October, 1912. The Young Turks had just promised considerable autonomy to the Albanians, and the Balkan allies rushed like wolves to grab portions of their poor little Balkan neighbour before there was time to delimit her frontiers and establish her. Russia tried vainly to stop them. Yougourieff, the Russian "officer who was training Montenegrin cadets at Cetinje, told me furiously that there must be no Balkan war till October, 1914, when Russia's preparations for her great war for Constantinople would be complete. He added that Russia could not begin unless Austria did. The Balkan war having begun, Russia at once

---

v The italics are mine.

safeguarded her interests by forbidding any Balkan people to set foot in Constantinople and notifying the Powers that in such case she would send the Black Sea fleet there.

Russia's plans required a Great Serbia. She was therefore reluctant to arbitrate when Serbia broke her pledge to Bulgaria and seized all Bulgarian Macedonia. The French Yellow Book on Balkan affairs during 1912-14[vi] shows how, even had Russia "arbitrated," it was planned that the judgment should be in favour of Serbia. Otherwise King Peter would have abdicated, and his son would have taken the throne and forcibly annexed the coveted districts. Russia dared not alienate the Serbs on whom she depended for her plans for 1914; Bulgaria was doomed. Russia rejoiced naively at the result of the second Balkan war. Izvolsky writes from Paris on August 14th, 1913[vii].

"Events have taken the most favourable course for us... Had Bulgaria come out victor, it would have been very disadvantageous and dangerous for us... A great Bulgaria might have served as a base for ulterior Bulgar plans against Constantinople."

Russia and France further strengthened Serbia by paring down Albania to the bone and giving the best lands to their ally. When the British Commissioner, Colonel Granet, tried to decide justly which were Albanian enclaves, he was furiously opposed by his two colleagues, who told him his business as one of the Entente was to give all to Serbia. As large a Serbia as possible having been made, France at Russia's request made a large loan to Serbia to enable her to get as soon as possible into fighting

---
vi *Documents Diplomatiques: Les Affaires Balkaniques, 1912-1914.* 3 Vols.
vii *Op. cit.*, Vol. II, p. 133.

trim. Thus, at the end of 1913, Russia's "historic mission" and her Pan-Slavonic schemes were nearer realisation than perhaps ever before. Serbia was her enthusiastic tool and Russia was pledged to regard any Austrian aggression as a *casus belli*. All that was needed was to make Austria "aggress." Through the months which followed, I never forgot that Yougourieff had said Russia would be ready in October, 1914, and could not begin unless Austria did; nor that the Montenegrins had added: "We shall begin in Bosnia." It all came true.

Two facts have balked Russia's well-laid plan. We failed to put her (at our own expense) into Constantinople, and the Russian revolution broke out. For both facts we must be devoutly thankful. Were Russia now in triumph at Constantinople and had not the revolution taken place, France and Russia would have partitioned Europe according to the nefarious treaty they made behind our backs in February, 1917, and we should be dancing on our hind-legs outside vainly begging for bits. Our position as it is, is none too strong.

France, ignoring her debt to us, is financing and arming the Slavonic block of Poles, Czechs and Serbs until Russia again takes the war-path. The Balkans, except Albania, are swarming with Russians who have boasted to friends of mine: "After all, we have taken the Balkans!" Russia has had high fever, but her convalescence, accompanied as is usual in such cases with a huge appetite, is but a matter of time. Judging by her "Red" programme, her desire to carry out her "historic mission" by giving her ideals to Europe is stronger than ever.

To counterbalance the new, great westward thrust of the Slav peoples we have nothing to show but a short toddle eastward into Slovenia by Italy. Italy knew her enemy was not the Teuton but the Slav, and made war only on the understanding she was to be allowed to bottle him up all along the Adriatic. A wild dream—unrealised. When the next east to west march is made, Trieste and Fiume will be among the first to fall. France, the one land whose falling population needed no accession of territory, has, it is true, advanced eastward into Alsace-Lorraine. But as this is a wholly short-skulled enclave, this may be reckoned as a further *westward* advance of the short-skulled people. By way of hastening the change of the race type of Europe, France is now importing Syrians and Armenians and settling them in France. Her policy with regard to her African troops is not calculated either to improve the population of Europe.

King Constantine's reluctance to allow his Greeks to help pull chestnuts from the fire for the Slav was perfectly sound. The Serb is consolidating his position in the annexed lands by expelling aliens and forcibly "Serbising" those that remain. What is the meaning of the tramp from east to west we do not know? Will the civilisation of the northern long-skulled people of Europe go down in a welter as did that of the Mediterranean people and be followed by a Dark Age? We know only that the northern long-skull has just made what was possibly his last desperate dash eastward and has failed, and that no march from west to east has as yet succeeded. Even the army of Alexander the Great was absorbed, and our own hold on India and Mesopotamia will never people them with Europeans.

We must recognise the fact that the march of the short-skulled people from the east continues and that we ourselves have helped to tear down the barriers which in all probability we can never replace. Our fate, if we are destined to survive, seems likely to be to find homes outside Europe. "Cain... What hast thou done? Thy brother's blood crieth to me from the ground... A fugitive and a wanderer shalt thou be on the earth."

[Resume of a paper read by Miss M. Edith Durham on April 1st, 1924. from: *Journal of the British Institute of International Affairs,* London, Vol. III, May 1924, p. 139-144.]

Tribes of Northern Albania

Of the new states which have arisen in Europe out of the wreckage of old empires the one which has been least understood and the most unlucky— for during the war, although her independence and neutrality had been guaranteed by all the powers, Albania was entered and more or less overrun by no less than seven armies—is Albania. But the history of the Albanian people is a very remarkable one, for few peoples have shown greater tenacity to their language and customs than have the Albanians. The Albanian represents those ancient inhabitants who filled the Balkans before the Roman invasion and conquest of the peninsula. Even the Roman was a long while subduing the Illyrian as he was then called. And the conquered native finally became a great force in the Roman army, and ultimately rose to the purple. Diocletian, Constantine the Great, Justinian and other emperors of lesser note had Balkan blood in them.

Christianity reached Illyria at a very early date. "Round about unto Illyricum have I fully preached the gospel of Christ," says St. Paul. The bishoprics of Albania are of ancient date.

Accursed Slavonians

Into this Christianized and partly Romanized land poured the Slavs, the latest comers of the Balkan peoples.

John of Ephesus gives a contemporary account of their first appearance. "The third year after Justinian was famous for the invasion of the accursed people called Slavonians... And four years have elapsed and because the king is engaged in war with the Persians... they spread far and wide and ravage and burn and take captives. They have ridden to the outer wall of the town (Byzantium) and driven away thousands of the king's horses and even to this day (A.D. 584) they still dwell free from fear and slay and burn... and have learned to fight better than the Romans, though at first they were rude savages and dared not show themselves outside the forests, and as for arms did not know them except for two or three kinds of javelins or darts."

Serbian Collapse

The Slav problem of the Near East then began. The struggle between the old inhabitant and the invader has never ceased.
A number of old documents relating to Serb rule in the Middle Ages show the Albanian in districts far wider than modern Albania, as serf or herdsman under the ruling Serb feudal nobleman. Serb kings hand over Albanian villages and mills as gifts to Serb monasteries and so forth.

And when the Serb kingdom fell to pieces in the 14th century, the Albanians were among the first to break loose.

Since then the Albanian has weathered also the Turkish storm. This remnant of an ancient people has retained its language and it's strong individuality against all comers.

Strabo, writing in the first century A.D., describes the Illyrians and Macedonians as divided into tribes and says "the persons who hold office are called *peligones*." Among the Albanian northern mountains the tribes still maintained semi-independence under Turkish rule, and each tribe managed its internal affairs by means of a council of elders. An old man in Albanian is *plak* or *pelak*, which is evidently the same word as Strabo's *pelig*—the termination "ones" being probably a Roman addition.

The Turkish conquest in many ways was as great a misfortune to the Albanian as to the other Balkan people. It broke the independent state made by the great Skenderbeg. But it later enabled the Albanian to retake much of the land which the Slav had taken from his ancestors. The Serb fled into Austria where he was protected and given land, and the Albanian reoccupied the lands he had left. The Albanian language spread as far as Monastir in Macedonia.

Had Lord Fitzmaurice and Lord Goschen, when in 1880 the Eastern Roumelian commission was regulating the results of the Russo-Turkish war of 1877, succeeded in their plan of forming a large autonomous Albania, by this time the Albanians would have been a strong power in the Balkans. But Great Powers who coveted Albanian lands did not permit this to be done. And when in 1913 Albania, after centuries of struggle, finally won recognition, she was shorn of some million inhabitants and some of her most fertile land and most important towns.

And during the war, though she was much devastated, no one has paid her reparations. Since the war, moreover, she has been more than once attacked and invaded by the Serbs. But so far the League of Nations has [not] stood her friend and ordered back the invaders.

Hard as has been her lot, the sturdy individualism of the Albanians gives hope that 'given time, they will yet play a part in the development of the Near East. In intelligence, as those who have travelled among them have found, they are second to none of the other Balkan peoples.

The Changing Age

The perpetual struggle to hold their own against all comers has naturally led the Albanian to guard jealously his old customs. In no other part of Europe, perhaps, has the Great War made such sweeping changes as in the Balkans, where the peoples have been jumped in many cases from the middle ages to the twentieth century without time to take breath.

Under the Turk, no schools, except such as were under foreign protection, were allowed to teach in Albanian. As this is the only tongue spoken by the bulk of the population, education was severely handicapped, though the schools opened by Austria and Italy were taken full advantage of.

But now the schoolmaster is abroad. The first thing done by the Albanians on obtaining independence was to open as many schools as their rather straitened means allowed.

The ancient beliefs and customs that lingered in the remote mountain fastnesses and are of extreme interest to all students of the past, will disappear more and more rapidly.

We will therefore touch on some of these rather than on the present political and other questions with the hope that some student of anthropology will be tempted to make further studies on the spot before the passing away of the older generation carries much old lore into oblivion.

Folklore and Customs

When I visited the northern tribes in Turkish times, the council of elders still ruled them. These elders were all House-lords (*zoti i shpis*) that is, heads of families. The families included a number of cousins and among the more isolated tribes such a family might amount to some sixty or more person. But smaller ones were usual. The headship was inherited from father to son by the eldest son, unless he were considered a quite incompetent person. The head was obeyed. I have seen a young man of not more than eight and twenty ordering his much older uncles. "But why do they obey him?" I asked. "Because he is the head appointed by God," I was told.

In such a place, one learns the meaning of the divine right of kings.

The council of elders decided all matters within the tribe—wood-felling rights, irrigation rights, pasturage, etc. In case of quarrels with another tribe it met delegates from that tribe and argued the point. The law was called the Canon of Lek Dukaghin after a celebrated chieftain of the 14th century, but was doubtless handed down from a far earlier time and rearranged or modified by Lek. It had also been modified by the elders of different districts in more recent days, and so was not the same in all tribes in certain details.

And it had never been written down till collected and written recently by Bishop Miédia and Don Kol Asti.

Theft within the tribe was punished by making the thief restore double what he had stolen and such theft was not common.

Theft from land that was church (in the case of the Catholic tribes) or mosque property (for the Moslems) was punished by the restoration of four or five time, the value. Part of the fine went to pay the expenses of the elders who often had to come long distance If a house or cattle-yard were broken into an extra fine of 500 piastres was payable. An accused man had to find con-jurors who would swear to his innocence. Not necessarily witnesses in our sense of the word. The number of con-jurors varied according (to the nature of the crime. A man accused of murder within the tribe had to find twenty-four. For theft of anything but livestock twelve. For horse-stealing, eight; for cattle stealing, six; for sheep or goats, two. And so forth.

For a murder within the tribe the murderer was expelled from the tribe, his ground confiscated, his house burnt and often his fruit trees felled. Some tribes gave the land to the relatives of the murdered man. A fine of some 3,000 piastres was also exacted.

In some tribes, blood vengeance within the tribe was not permitted. In others, the relatives might take blood if they did so at once on the first day.

In the case of the murder of a member of another tribe, that tribe might take vengeance.

Blood Tax

As the Turkish government always took part of the fines paid for murder, it rather encouraged the taking of vengeance as a source of revenue. Now efforts are being made with success to put an end to an ancient and bad custom, and it will soon become a thing of the past as in other lands?

In the case of wounds, fines were exacted in proportion to the wound. In making peace after a feud, it was customary for the Elders to reckon up the injuries on both sides. Thus a death on one side was balanced by one on the other. And so were wounds. For the balance, fines had to be paid no matter which party started the quarrel. A system which is far more just than the system of "reparations" in force in the rest of Europe, where the victor may extort what he can.

These tribes were and are strictly exogamous. That is, that no marriage could take place within the tribe which reckons descent from one male ancestor. In tribes which include two unrelated stocks intermarriage of those stocks can take place.

A very ancient custom which was not yet extinct when I visited the tribes was that in the more remote region of the Dukaghin tribes, the Levirate was still practised in spite of the efforts of the priests to suppress it. On the decease of a tribesman, it was held the duty of his brother or, failing a brother, his nearest male relative, to marry the widow, even if he had already a wife. I came across several cases. But the custom is probably now extinct. I remember that of a young man who was deeply distressed because the priest had excommunicated him and all his household on account of such a marriage. In this case he had no other wife. He repeatedly said that he could not promise to put her away as bidden, for it was a duty he owed to his brother. The woman was childless, and it appeared that a child born to her later would rank as that of the dead man. As it did in Old Testament days.

The ancient cult of the hearth also was not extinct among these people. Among the Pulati people when a new house was built, the first fire had to be ceremonially lit by the house lord who had to enter the house nude. When the fire was lighted, the rest of the household could enter.

I was told that the fire was ceremonially extinguished by the women if the last male of the house died. As a rule, the hearth fire being of wood and banked up always at night, was not extinguished for years.

Voyage of the Soul

At death, the soul was believed to come from the mouth and walk three times round the corpse before departing. It then had to travel back to the place at which it was born, visiting on the way every place in turn in which the man had ever been during his life. After this, which might take years, the soul conformed either to Christian or Moslem custom, according to its beliefs during life in this world.

Both Christian and Moslem tribesmen seemed to think heaven was on the summit of an immensely high mountain.

The name tabu—the desire to conceal a person's name lest evil spells be worked with it—a tabu to be found in very many lands, was not extinct. Women refused to mention the name of their husband. I was told it was not modest to do so. Their trouble when asked for the name was very marked. They would even burst into tears. And when, while doing relief work after war, it was necessary to make accurate lists of refugees, such names had to be obtained from other women.

Among the men in some districts it was customary not to use the baptismal name, but to adopt another for use on growing up. A custom combatted by the priests, but stuck to with some pertinacity.

As in other primitive places, there was, of course, a widespread belief both in the evil eye and in witches, and magicians. Of the latter I was told a tale which the tellers believed firmly. A certain magician did so much harm by his spells that the local Pasha imprisoned him. He languished some time in prison till one festival day the Pasha was entertaining guests. The party was a very dull one, and by way of enlivening it, some one suggested that the imprisoned magician should be released to entertain the company. No sooner said than done. The magician was willing to oblige, and all the apparatus he needed was a large bowl of water. This was fetched and he asked the company what foreign town they would like to see in it. Someone suggested Malta. The magician after performing a little magic asked the company to look in the bowl. There, sure enough, was the port of Malta, all the houses, people and ships clearly visible. Alongside the quay was a large steamer getting up steam and preparing to cast off. "Noble Pasha," said the magician, "have I your permission to go away in the ship?"

"Certainly," said the Pasha much amused. The magician solemnly lifted his foot and put it on board the steamer in the water bowl. And he disappeared and was never seen more.

That he steamed away from Malta in the ship is clear to the meanest intelligence.

The future is told from the blade bones of sheep and the breast bones of fowls. Remnants of the ancient Greek and Roman prophecies by means of animals possibly. The bone is held against the light and the markings made by the marrow and the situation of little holes or white patches are interpreted by those who know the lore.

The last time I heard a bone read it came fatally true. It was in June, 1914, on the shore at Durazzo. Among a crowd of officials and foreigners down by the quay there came in search of me a ragged lean man from the distant mountains. He drew a fowl's breast-bone from his shirt and held it against the sun-glare very anxiously and asked my opinion.

He said, "I see blood. Nothing but blood. Blood everywhere. What can it mean?" Some educated Albanians laughed at him. But he persisted. I remember his eager dark eyes and his anxious face and the little bone which shone crimson in the sun. And alas he was right. But a few weeks saw the Great War. And blood was everywhere.

To those who have the enterprise to go to Albania to collect the ancient lore that still remains, I would say that though a certain amount of roughing it must be put up with, the welcome that the traveller meets with makes up for it. The scenery of the mountains is second to none in Europe and the climber may climb unknown peaks.

Every sympathetic traveller who visits Albania is a help to a brave people which is faced with difficulties.

And those who would search for the remains of the old world lore of Europe should go before the exploiters and concessionaire who are hovering over the land have got their claws into it.

[from: *Discovery: a Monthly Popular Journal of Knowledge,* London, Vol. 62, February 1925.]

A Very Free Press

Recently a correspondent in your columns drew attention to the humours and drawbacks of a strictly censored Press in Japan. Perhaps, by way of contrast, the results of an absolutely Free Press, under which I once suffered, may not come amiss. It was in Scutari-Albania, immediately after the Young Turk revolution of 1908. There was extraordinary enthusiasm. The air buzzed with Liberty, Equality and Fraternity. In future everyone would do just as he pleased. The more optimistic declared all prisons would be abolished and the reign of Justice begin.

The Press, which had been so severely fettered that it scarcely existed, was let loose. And a rumour spread that Scutari would shortly have a paper of its own, published by a certain Mr. P——.

P—— was a well-known character—a Jew who had turned Moslem. His father had been a pharmacist, possessed, it was said, of medical skill and respected in the town. From him P—— had inherited the pharmacy—now indescribably filthy—and was supposed also to have inherited the knowledge. At any rate he was deemed a skilful veterinary, sold pills and

Epsom salts to humans, and was a noted linguist.

Late one evening there came a knocking at my outer gate and I was told Mr. P—— and a lady had called on business. In came P——. He wore neither shirt nor socks, but, as he had previously explained to me that he preferred this form of attire, I was not surprised. He was followed by a draggled and melancholy female, whom he introduced as "a kind of relation" and ordered to sit down. She obeyed, and he remarked cheerfully: "I, as you know, am a Moslem. I therefore take coffee only. But she is a Christian, so would like a glass of wine." The rites of hospitality having been fulfilled, P—— explained his errand somewhat as follows: "No doubt you have heard I am about to publish a paper. The printing-press has only just arrived, but I hope to get the first number out next week and have come to ask you to patronise it. You will find it worth while, for it will start a new era in journalism. Till now papers have usually been called *The Daily This* and *The Daily That*. Now, any fool can find out what happens in the day. What is really interesting is to know what people do after dark. This town seethes with political intrigues, as you know. I have arranged a service of disguised spies who will watch the doors of all the Foreign Consulates at night and of all the chief personages in the town. I assure you the news will be of great interest."

Having received my promise of support, P—— and draggled female departed. And in a few days out came the paper. It was called *The Sun*. P—— wrote and printed it entirely himself in seldom less than four languages and two or three different types, including Turkish. Free indeed it was. It was outspoken, scurrilous, indecent, and almost always funny. It bubbled with verse in any language. It attacked boldly all the Great Powers and libelled their Royal Families in ribald rhymes each more unspeakable than the last. And in turn each Consul and Vice-Consul arose in wrath, strode to the Governor of the town, and protested on behalf of the Government he represented, only to be met with the Governor's polite regret that, though the incident was deplorable, he could do nothing : "We have Freedom of the Press." Each Consul cursed in turn and secretly enjoyed the attack next week on another Government. But the result of his own complaint usually was that a worse accusation against him or his Government appeared soon after.

Then there was a conjoint protest of the Powers, and they wrung from the Governor a promise that *The Sun* should cease. So it did. It came out next week as *The Moon,* livelier than ever.

Up till now Great Britain had been spared by P——. Now, by way of variety, he devoted a whole column to abuse of me, which was ungrateful of him. It was a nasty article. One of the minor charges was that I lived on the proceeds of a brothel. Round came our old British Vice-Consul in a fury. He was an Albanian, a good old man, devoted to Great Britain, and he was pained and horrified. With my consent he proposed to go at once to the Governor to lodge a protest. "No," said I, "don't. All the Powers have protested in vain and P—— in delighted. Say nothing at all and he will be disappointed. Everyone knows the article is untrue. It won't hurt me." And we said nothing. Rather to my surprise the next number and the next contained no mention of me. I met P—— in the main street and called out. "Hallo, P——, how are you getting on?" He stared at me for an instant, and then bolted like a rabbit up the nearest bye-street, followed by the laughter of the bystanders. His obvious terror astonished me.

Then, under seal of secrecy, the mystery was explained. I had many friends among the mountain tribesmen. When they heard of the attack upon me they were furious. A chosen band came down at night, entered P——'s house, thrashed him, and gave him the fright of his life. Next time another word against me appeared they would flog him to death. Poor P——! He really did learn then "what happens at night." And when I hailed him in the street, he though I had a band of stalwarts waiting round the corner.

I kept the secret. Every Consul in turn wanted to know what I had done to suppress P—— so completely. I replied truthfully: "Nothing at all." P—— continued his attacks upon them and I remained immune.

But pride has a fall. P——, emboldened by months of success, attacked the Young Turk Government. And was expelled from the country—or fled for his life, I do not know which—in twenty-four hours. Freedom of the Press was no protection this time. It was a case of Defence of the Realm.

I heard that P—— reached Trieste and never heard of him again. He was a clever little devil. But too much Freedom is not really good for anyone.

[from: *The New Statesman and Nation*, London, May 2, 1931.]

The Making of a Saint

Chance has thrown into my hands a pamphlet published at Cetinje, Montenegro, containing a number of State documents recently discovered in the palace of the late King Nikola. Among them is the original Proclamation of the sainthood of Vladika (Bishop) Petar I, the King's great-great uncle, who died on 19th October, 1830.

It is still customary among many members of the Eastern Orthodox Church to open the grave from three to four years after burial—at such time when the corpse may be reasonably expected to have decayed—cleanse the bones and store them in an ossuary. And in many places until quite recently it was customary to put food upon the grave and hold funeral feasts at stated intervals so long as the body remained in the grave: a custom possibly not yet extinct. I found it flourishing thirty years ago,

In the rare cases in which the corpse has become mummified, the fact is looked on as a miraculous sign that life everlasting among the saints has been attained and the corpse is accordingly venerated. This was the case with Bishop Petar Petrovitch I.

The pamphlet is entitled "Spomenica"; it is edited by Dushan Vuksan and printed at Cetinje, 1926. The passage in question runs as follows:

"The proclamation of the Metropolitan Petar I as a Saint."
The Proclamation of Vladika Radé (his popular name) in which it is told that the body of Petar I was disinterred on 18th October, 1834, and on that occasion was found to be quite complete, was printed in Cetinje in 1834. But whether this Proclamation, which was made "to the whole nation of Montenegro and the Brda," went beyond the frontiers of Montenegro, is unknown to me (the Editor).

I found in the archives of the Palace in the fascicle of the year 1834 one single copy of this Proclamation and herewith publish it in entirety. It is printed on blue paper of large format and on it is the autograph signature of the Vladika (Petar II). The Proclamation announces:

"From our Vladika, Petar Petrovitch, to the whole nation of Montenegro and the Brda[viii] a proclamation and a greeting.
We give ye to know, oh Godfearing nation, how we, on the 18th of this month on St. Luke's Day did open the blessed grave of my holy Predecessor and your Archpriest (Arhipastir) Petar. And when we had opened the grave, we found complete the holy body of our Archpriest.

Therefore, oh Godfearing nation, joyfully do we proclaim to you this fortunate event; for we know that ye will give thanks to the Omnipotent Creator who has sent among you the good

---

viii Brda: a group of partly Albanian mountain tribes, annexed to Montenegro in the 18th century and now slavized.

father and mighty pastor of the Church and the Christian flock, your protector and saviour, in his complete body. That, just as when in his mortal body he was ready to give his soul and body for you, so now we pray to him that, as a Saint and one favoured by God, he will pray to Almighty God for us as for his own sons.

I think, oh Godfearing Christians, that ye remember the words of St. Petar who said to you: 'May ye live in accord and peace and unity.' I think that every one of you has kept these holy and godly words in his heart since this man, so beloved of God, no longer lived among you.

And now I hope especially that you will keep them, for you see him that spoke them is amongst you, sainted and complete. And you are assured—I think—that if any Montenegrin will not preserve accord, peace and unity, St. Petar will be his accuser both in this world and in the other; but let those that have enmity between them (i.e., bloodfeud) agree and make peace and thus they will be pleasing both to God and your Sainted Petar.

Recommending you to God and His favourite and newly proclaimed Saint I remain,
to each of you the well wisher,

Vladika of Montenegro and the Brda,
Petar Petrovitch.
St. Luke's Day, Cetinje, 1834."

St. Petar Petrovitch was deeply revered by the Montenegrin peasants who almost always swore "By God and St. Peter." And, in fact, did not distinguish him from the great St. Peter. I have seen men strike their heads against his tomb and even against the door jambs of the Monastery church where he lies.

The other popular saint of Montenegro, St. Basil of Ostrog, a bishop who fled from Turkish persecution and lived in a cave in the mountain side at Ostrog, likewise derived his sainthood from the fact that his body was found to be intact. When I made the pilgrimage to this shrine, the body was packed in carbolized cotton wool. One foot was uncovered for me to kiss.

Such saints, I believe, are purely local and almost unknown to other branches of the Orthodox Church.

The Vladika of Montenegro had no temporal power. Such government as existed in his time was purely tribal and conducted by the tribal headmen. The Vladika's power, which was very considerable, consisted in his power of blessing and banning. His curse was greatly dreaded and, if we may believe local tradition, it was most efficacious and the stern old man applied it freely.

Thus, being wrath with a recalcitrant tribesman he said "I wish you may die." The man contracted smallpox and died soon after.

Again, the Vladika owned fishing rights in the lake and the fishermen had to supply a tribute of fish to the monastery. None arrived. The Vladika asked, why? The fishers replied that they had been unable to catch any. Time passed and still no fish. Again the Vladika asked and was told "there are no fish in the lake." "No," said he firmly, "there are none and there never will be any more." And there were no more, till the terrified fishermen implored the Vladika to remove the curse and promised a plentiful supply of fish in the future.

As the fish in the Lake of Scutari are extremely plentiful

at certain seasons and slacken between whiles, we can only suppose the holy man timed his curse skilfully.

The skilful use made by his nephew and successor, Vladika Petar II, of the fact of the canonization, in order to stop the blood feuds which raged between the tribes at this period, should be noted.

The Proclamation of 1834 is perhaps the last instance of sainthood by natural mummification. But how deeply rooted the idea is in the minds of peoples brought up in the Orthodox Church is shown by the immense reverence paid by the Russian people to the artificially embalmed body of Lenin. The tradition lives, though times have changed.

[from: *Man, Journal of the Royal Anthropological Society,* London, September 1933, p. 146-147.]

Albania

The Albanians are the descendants of the tribes of Illyrians and Epirots, who, in prehistoric times, inhabited all the western side of the Balkan Peninsula from Trieste in the north to the Gulf of Arta in the south. They are now known as the Ghegs and the Tosks, and form a united nation. Strabo, writing at the beginning of the Christian era, when they had fallen under Roman rule, gives a detailed account of them, showing that their tribal system was in many ways like that which existed in the mountains until recent days.

Modern Albania comprises a very small portion of the Albanians' former lands. Her more powerful neighbours, especially during the Balkan wars of 1912-13 and the war of 1914-18, have annexed large districts that were wholly Albanian, and, though, in 1912, Albania was at last recognised by the Powers as an independent and neutral state, she was shorn of much of what should have been her most valuable lands, Greeks and Serbs taking them.

Albania, as an independent state, extends from Scutari in the north to Butrinto in the south, roughly speaking, with a large mountainous hinterland. The rivers thus run mainly from east to west. The plain lands all along the coast are extremely fertile, as the soil is all formed of the detritus brought down by the rivers, which, when the winter snows melt, are torrential, though their beds are often nearly dry in summer. As during the centuries when the land was under Turkish rule, the rivers were in no way regulated, the immense amount of silt brought down has in some cases, as at Medua, formed a bar at the river mouth, and, in others, rendered the bays so shallow that no large vessel could approach the shore. From the accounts now given of the bombing of the "ports" of Durazzo and Valona, it appears that the Italians must have put an immense amount of work into harbour-making. Owing to this silting of the river mouths, the land around them had become waterlogged, and a bad form of malaria was rampant, making some parts uninhabitable in summer. They, however, formed excellent pasture and farm lands for the winter.

The mountain tribes who dwell in the high mountains all own winter lands on the plains. In autumn and in spring—on St. George's Day—the migration of thousands of men, women and children and their flocks was a sight never to be forgotten. It was often a four or five days' march, especially in spring when the air resounded with the bleating of hundreds of new-born lambs, kids and calves, not to mention the squalls of infants slung in wooden cradles on their mothers' backs. Slowly, slowly the seemingly endless procession wound through Scutari and up the stony tracks to the high mountains, where most of the tribesmen had their homes.

Each tribe owned a large tract of land, the frontiers of which were strictly defined. The tribes, when under the Turks, which was when I knew them, preserved a form of local autonomy. Each was governed by a Council of Elders (*Pelaki*). An Elder was the headman of a "house" (*shpi*), and a "house" consisted of a family group which might extend to second cousins all living together either in one building or in a group of houses, but all ruled by the Elder—the House Lord. The Council of Elders administered the unwritten ancient law of the mountains, a rough form of justice. A theft within the tribe was punished by making the thief restore double what he had taken. For theft from church land ten times the amount must be restored. Expulsion from the tribe was the severest form of punishment. In the case of murder, the nearest male relatives of the dead man had the duty of avenging him. The Elders also regulated all pasture, forest and water rights. A certain amount of each was allotted to each "house," and no one might graze beasts or fell timber except in his own portion. In times of drought, the water was strictly regulated.

These mountain men, by what seems inherited lore, were extraordinarily skilful in carrying water from high springs for miles along little canals formed along the mountain side and conducted across valleys in pipes made of hollowed tree trunks. They had no apparatus by which to measure levels, but made surprisingly good aqueducts. From these main waterways, small trenches were cut across the small fields where the mountain men grew some maize, onions and cabbages. The water was also made to fall through a wooden pipe from a height on to the turbine wheels of the small corn-mills that were dotted about the mountains. The mills sometimes were property of the tribe, and in that case anyone could grind his own corn there. If privately owned, the miller took some flour as payment. Such mills were common all over Europe at one time.

The tribesman's house was built of the local stone. A great part of the northern mountains (Maltsia e Madhe = Great Mountains) is of limestone. The typical house of a well-to-do family had very thick walls, sometimes unmortared, roofed with slabs of stone. Below was the stable, and store-room, harness, ploughs, etc. Above lived the family, often in one vast room, or a space divided into two or three. There was no ceiling. The fire was on a big open hearth, and the smoke found its way out through a hole in the gable wall. Wood only was burnt, and the fire never allowed to go out. Banked up at night, a handful of dry leaves and fanning with a fowl's wing roused it again in the morning. The ashes were carefully collected for washing clothes; as the ashes are strongly alkaline, clothes boiled with them are quickly cleansed, and, dried on grass in the sun, become finely bleached.

The main source of a living in the mountains is the flocks—sheep and goats for the most part, and small cattle, herded mainly by the men, who also cultivate the land. Sheep milk was preferred to cow milk, and milk was the main food of the mountain people. They took it either boiled and hot, from a vast iron cauldron, or soured (*kos*). Raw milk was rarely drunk. The sour milk was the favourite food, and that and maize bread formed the staple food. Meat was eaten mainly on feast days. It was too valuable for everyday use. On weekly market days the man trudged down to Scutari, perhaps a three days' march, with sheep and goats, and bartered them for goods or sold them for cash. As the mountains could not grow enough maize, most of this had to be bought. The mountains also supplied the towns with firewood and charcoal.

Women's work was very heavy. They had to make all the

bread, which was baked on the hot hearth-stone under an iron cover on which hot ashes were heaped. They began bread-making at four in the morning. They had to fetch all the water and firewood, look after the fowls, milk the sheep and goats, make the sour milk, and spin and weave the thick woollen stuff for clothing of both men and women. The spinning was done on a flat distaff, often well chip-carved. Whenever a woman was not bread-making or washing or otherwise using her hands, she spun perpetually. Black sheep were valued as much as white sheep, for black and white stripes were woven, and the black wool also plaited to make the braid with which the men's costumes were lavishly trimmed. Different tribes used different patterns. The loom was of wood, and could be taken to pieces and carried and set up anywhere. When woven, the cloth was taken to a fulling mill on a river, and there hammered under water by heavy wooden mallets till it formed a thick and nearly indestructible felt. The women also helped with both cultivation and herding.

So much for the mountains. The plains near the towns, where high enough above the malarial parts, are extremely fertile. Vegetables of many kinds grew almost while you watched them. Pumpkins, potatoes, tomatoes, wax beans, aubergines, lettuces, onions, leeks in great variety, flourished in the market gardens and were brought to the bazaar. On the lower slopes of the mountains, chestnut trees flourished, so did walnuts and hazel nuts. There were also many fine olive gardens, but a number of these were destroyed by Montenegrins in the Balkan war of 1912. The figs and cherries were the finest I have ever come across. Grapes, too, were plentiful, and some of the local wine was very good.

All along the plains of the coast the land is similarly fertile. But here much of it was and is owned by wealthy (for Albania) Beys, who, in many cases, neglected to cultivate it. It was worked on the Turkish *chiftlik* system, in which the landowner has to provide the housing, implements and other necessaries for farming, and the labourer has to give him a large proportion of all crops, etc., and is unpaid save for the produce he is allowed to keep—a system which can be satisfactory or not according to what the landlord is like. Certain Beys boasted that they were so rich that they need not bother to have all their land cultivated. Thus much good land was wasted. And there, as in other lands, the peasants have wanted small holdings.

Formerly there was a large amount of silk grown in Albania, and buyers from Italy came to Scutari. But the silkworm disease which swept over South Europe in the 19th century inflicted such damage that the trade diminished and only a small amount of silk for home use was cultivated. In the towns of Albania this was handwoven in many a house into a variety of very fine and beautiful tissues, and used for the handsome costumes of both Christian and Moslem ladies. Much of the costumes for festive occasions were richly embroidered with gold thread. The raised gold work, in both design and craftsmanship, has rarely, if ever, been surpassed. The gold embroidery and that in coloured braids were mainly the work of men. Women embroidered the many scarves, guest towels, bedspreads, etc., which formed part of a bride's outfit. The silversmiths, too, brought their work to high perfection. Though working with the simplest tools over a little charcoal fire, astonishingly fine and beautiful work was made. And in old days the stocks and barrels of pistols and guns were inlaid or formed of hammered silver. Unfortunately, as in other lands, these beautiful home industries are fast disappearing before the rush of trashy and cheap machine-made goods from abroad. But they show the Albanian to be the artist of the Balkans.

Houses in the towns were mostly built of stone, not more than two storeys high, and for the most part roofed with red tiles. Within they are very clean. Handsome hand-woven carpets hang on the walls and cover divans. As streets in the rainy season are very muddy, it is usual to leave dirty shoes on the doorstep. There are usually no bedrooms. When bedtime comes, mattresses are taken from a cupboard and spread on the floor; and a large cover wadded with cottonwool serves as blanket.

Food in the towns was plentiful and very varied. Highly flavoured dishes with plenty of paprika, pilaffs of rice, stuffed aubergines, and much game were popular. Snipe, woodcock and hares, and quantities of wild duck from the lakes were brought into the bazaars by the peasants. If you took your own dish to the cook shop, you could carry home three or four pennyworth of all manner of foods. Of timber there was plenty in the mountains—fine beech forests and, higher up, fir and pine. But much of the forest-land had been spoiled by the ignorant tribesmen, who in order to obtain more pasture-land for flocks, burnt large patches, with the fatal result that the soil, deprived of the roots which bound it, was washed down into the rivers by the torrential rains of autumn and the thawing of the winter snows, leaving the underlying rock completely denuded. Another fatal practice was that of allowing goats to feed on young growing trees which, though they survived the process, were too much deformed to be used as timber.

Nevertheless, there is still much fine forest-land, which needs only care to be a lasting source of profit.

When I lived in Albania there were no made roads except in the towns and their immediate neighbourhood. All transport was by means of pack-saddles. Small tough horses and mules clambered over the roughest stony tracks with great skill and sure-footedness. Smaller packs were carried by women. Rivers were crossed in ferry boats made of two dug-out tree trunks lashed together. On the river Drin at Berisha the very ancient method of crossing the river on inflated sheep skins was still practised. I think I am about the only English person who has crossed a rapidly rushing river on a hurdle with four inflated sheep skins lashed to it—an exciting experience! Such was the life in Albania till recent times.

Albania exported, mainly into Italy, tobacco of which much of good quality is grown all through Albania. As there was no tax on it, the smuggling of it into neighbour lands was highly profitable. The roots of the sumach tree for dyeing and tanning leather, dried hides, the acorns of Valona also for tanning, and olive oil were other exports. Such was the simple life of the people—a hardy and intelligent race, whose one desire was to be free of foreign rule. In this all were united, both Moslem and Christian.

The Christians of the north are Roman Catholics. Some tribes are mixed Catholic and Moslem, for the Albanian is first of all an Albanian, and church law took a second place if it conflicted with old national custom. The Albanians of the north were converted early to Christianity and came under the rule of the Roman Patriarchate. The Christians of the south belong to the Eastern Orthodox Church and, since the land became independent, have succeeded in fulfilling a long-cherished desire and established legally the autocephalous Albanian Orthodox Church, and so freed themselves from Greek influence.

When Albania obtained independence, many other reforms were started, but since Italy got her claws into the land and continually tightened her grip, it has been almost impossible to learn what has been happening. That Italy must have seized much land for military purposes, stores, hangars, fortifications, is obvious. And many an Albanian must have seen his lands cut up by military and other roads. The plunge from almost mediaeval conditions to the mechanised life of to-day has been cruelly abrupt. The Albanians are a very intelligent people, and have hastened to take advantage of all educational opportunities offered them. Under the Turks their development was greatly hampered by the fact that the Turkish Government prohibited the printing and teaching of the Albanian language under severe penalties.

Few peoples have struggled to independence through more difficulties. I first learned of Albania's struggle in 1904. A very able Albanian—George Kyrias—an employee of the British and Foreign Bible Society, prepared certain books of the Bible in Albanian, and the Society published them. The Society had permission to sell its publications through the Turkish Empire. But the Turks had not reckoned on Albanian books. I was invited to accompany an Albanian colporteur who was to try to sell these books through the length of Albania. The object of the Albanian nationalist movement was to free the land of foreign influence. I joined the colporteur at his home at Liaskovik, and the first town I visited was Koritza. Here the sister of George Kyrias, a very able and brave woman, was head of a girls' school under the protection of the American Mission. She was trained in America and used American textbooks, but gave her lessons in Albanian, and all writing was destroyed after the lesson. The Turks searched in vain for the forbidden language. Girls, both Christian and Moslem, flocked to the school, learned to read and write, and taught their brothers. Koritza was the centre of the Albanian independence movement in the south. The school worked to counteract the influence of the Greek school and of Greek priests, whose presence was permitted by the Turks in order to check the growing national spirit of the Albanians. Miss Kyrias' school was called the Beacon Light.

For many weeks we rode and walked through Albania. There were no made roads then. We forded rivers where the horses almost swam, and plunged through marshes where the horses were bogged and had to be hauled and dug out. We visited all the chief towns. Wherever there was an Albanian Governor we were welcome to sell all the books we could. At Berati, where there was a Turk, we were arrested and brought before him. He said he had no objection to Christianity. We might sell as many gospels in French as we pleased, but not in Albanian; and he confiscated them all. It did not matter, as we had a store awaiting us ahead. It was an inspiring journey. Moslems as well as Christians hastened to buy books in their own language. "Now," said a young gendarme, "I can teach my young brother to read." I learned at Berati of the movement, then beginning, to form an autocephalous Orthodox Albanian Church, and so free the south from the influence of Greek priests. It was complained that the Greek priest informed against persons possessing Albanian books. After Albania became independent, the Albanian Church was established, and is now on a par with the Serb and Bulgar and Roumanian Churches, which are all autocephalous.

In Scutari, education was obtained by means of the schools established and protected by Austria and Italy, each of which coveted Albania, and, like the spider, tried to induce the Albanian "to walk into my parlour." So there were boys' and girls' schools, a technical school, and a boarding school for mountain boys, all financed by one or the other Great Power. The enthusiasm for education was amazing. An Albanian I knew was shocked to hear that in England boys were allowed to play games at schools. This, he thought, was very wrong, as at school you should give all your time to learning. And how eagerly they learned! When at last, in 1912, after the Balkan wars, Albania, shorn of much land, was declared independent, the opening of schools was one of the first things done. In this, Albania received much help from America, especially from Mr. Charles Crane, of Chicago.

But Albania had hardly been given time to find her feet when the war of 1914-18 broke out, and the unfortunate land was over-run by Serb, Montenegrin, French, Italian, Austrian and British troops. Serb and Greek endeavoured to partition it between them. Again the Powers intervened, and Albania was restored to independence. For a time all seemed to be going well. Fan Noli, the brave priest who led the movement for an autocephalous Albanian Church, was one of Albania's leading men and a candidate for the Presidency. He was of opinion that it were better for Albania to go slowly and to remain poor for a time than to fall into debt to a foreign power and to grant foreign concessions. He favoured cultivating the home lands and giving land to the peasants.

Oil was the undoing of Albania. It was believed to exist in large quantities. Fan Noli was reluctant to give concessions. His rival for the Presidency, Ahmed Bey Zogu, now known as King Zog, on the other hand, favoured getting rich quickly. He promised a large concession to the Anglo-Persian Oil Co. and one to Italy. He gained the support of the British Government, and the Anglo-Persian started boring. At this time Elizabeth, Lady Carnarvon, was doing a noble work for Albania in memory of her son, Colonel Aubrey Herbert, who was one of Albania's great champions. She equipped a hospital at Valona, started the very popular Boy Scout movement, started anti-malarial work in the swamps, and built and equipped a library. British officers were appointed to train the gendarmerie. All seemed hopeful. Alas! The Anglo-Persian found no oil worth working. It withdrew.

The Italians, on the contrary, found good oil in their concession. Great Britain had no further interest in Albania and recognised the country as Italy's sphere of interest. British influence was soon squeezed out. The Boy Scouts were first suppressed and finally the British officers were dismissed. Italy dug her claws in more and more deeply. The Albanians viewed with dismay the loss of their hard-won independence. Men of the younger generation, educated abroad, strove to stem the increasing power of Italy, but were harshly suppressed. Then came the fatal Good Friday, when we all looked on and allowed a huge mechanised force to overwhelm the small country, with the results from which we are suffering now, and Albania yet more!

She is now the battlefield of two rival powers, and

threatened with ruin in a quarrel which is not her own. She dreads of all things loss of more territory, as that would leave her too small to exist. She hopes for complete restoration, free from any foreign rule. On what a chance may the fate of a nation depend! Had the oil concession granted to Italy been allotted to the Anglo-Persian Co., Albania's lot now would be very different. She would not have been used as a jumping-off ground for the further conquests of a megalomaniac, but would have been able to develop on her own lines, slowly. There is ample space in the Balkans for all its peoples. It is to be hoped that, having survived for so many centuries and recovered from so many conquests, Albania will be allowed to rise again when the tempest of war has passed over her, and that her neighbours will not grudge her her fair share of territory.

[from: *Geography*, Manchester, Vol. 26, March 1941, p. 18-24.]

Bibliography

ALLCOCK, John B. & YOUNG, Antonia (ed.). *Black Lambs and Grey Falcons: Women Travelling in the Balkans*. New York & Oxford: Berghahn Books, 2000 274pp.

DURHAM, Mary Edith. *Through the Lands of the Serb.* London: Edward Arnold, 1904. 345pp.

———. *The Burden of the Balkans.* London: Edward Arnold, 1905. 331 pp.

———. *High Albania.* London: Edward Arnold, 1909, reprints 1970, 1985, 2000. 352pp.

———. *The Struggle for Scutari. Turk, Slav and Albanian.* London: Edward Arnold, 1914. 320pp.

———. *Twenty Years of Balkan Tangle.* London: George Allen & Unwin, 1920. 295pp.

———. *Die slawische Gefahr: zwanzig Jahre Balkan-Erinnerungen* von M. Edith Durham. Deutsch herausgegeben von Hermann Lutz. Dritte Auflage. Stuttgart: Robert Lutz, s.d. [post 1923]. 356pp.

———. *Venti anni di groviglio balcanico.* Tradotto da Stefania Pelli-Bossi. Florence: Felice Le Monnier, 1923, reprint Lecce: Argo 1994? viii + 341pp.

———. *The Serajevo Crime.* London: Edward Arnold, 1925.

———. *Some Tribal Origins, Laws and Customs of the Balkans.* Illustrated by the author. London: Allen & Unwin, 1928. reprint AMS 1979. 318pp.

———. *Njëzet vjet ngatëresa ballkanike.* Shqipëruar nga inglishtia prej S. Toto. Tirana: Mesagjeritë Shqiptare, 1944, reprint Tirana: Argeta LMG, 2001. 289pp.

———. *Brenga e Ballkanit dhe vepra të tjera për Shqipërinë dhe Shqiptarët.* Tirana: 8 Nëntori, 1990, reprint Tirana: Naum Veqilharxhi, 1998. 586pp.

———. *Durch das Land der Helden und Hirten: Balkanreisen zwischen 1900 und 1908*. Edition Frauenfahrten. Herausgegeben und aus dem Englischen übersetzt von Ingrid Steiner und Dardan Gashi. Vienna: Promedia, 1995. 221pp.

———. *Brenga e Ballkanasve*. Përkthyer nga origjinali Haris Thanasi. Përgatitur për botim L. & M. Gëzhilli. Tirana: Argeta, 1998. 352 pp.

———. *Albania and the Albanians: Selected Articles and Letters, 1903-1944*. Introduction by Harry Hodgkinson. Edited by Bejtullah Destani. London: Centre for Albanian Studies, 2001. 261pp.

ELSIE, Robert. *Historical Dictionary of Albania*. Second Edition. Historical Dictionaries of Europe, No. 75. Lanham, Toronto & Plymouth: Scarecrow Press, 2010. lxxiii + 587pp.

———. *Biographical Dictionary of Albanian History*. London: I.B. Tauris, 2013.

GOWING, Elizabeth. *Edith and I: on the Trail of an Edwardian Traveller in Kosovo*. Cornwall: Elbow Publishing, 2013. 280pp.

TANNER, Marcus. *Albania's Mountain Queen: Edith Durham and the Balkans*. London: I. B. Tauris, 2014. 304pp.